BEADLE'S DIME NATIONAL SPEAKER

LECTOR HOUSE PUBLIC DOMAIN WORKS

This book is a result of an effort made by Lector House towards making a contribution to the preservation and repair of original classic literature. The original text is in the public domain in the United States of America, and possibly other countries depending upon their specific copyright laws.

In an attempt to preserve, improve and recreate the original content, certain conventional norms with regard to typographical mistakes, hyphenations, punctuations and/or other related subject matters, have been corrected upon our consideration. However, few such imperfections might not have been rectified as they were inherited and preserved from the original content to maintain the authenticity and construct, relevant to the work. The work might contain a few prior copyright references as well as page references which have been retained, wherever considered relevant to the part of the construct. We believe that this work holds historical, cultural and/or intellectual importance in the literary works community, therefore despite the oddities, we accounted the work for print as a part of our continuing effort towards preservation of literary work and our contribution towards the development of the society as a whole, driven by our beliefs.

We are grateful to our readers for putting their faith in us and accepting our imperfections with regard to preservation of the historical content. We shall strive hard to meet up to the expectations to improve further to provide an enriching reading experience.

Though, we conduct extensive research in ascertaining the status of copyright before redeveloping a version of the content, in rare cases, a classic work might be incorrectly marked as not-in-copyright. In such cases, if you are the copyright holder, then kindly contact us or write to us, and we shall get back to you with an immediate course of action.

HAPPY READING!

BEADLE'S DIME NATIONAL SPEAKER

VARIOUS

ISBN: 978-93-90294-81-7

Published: -

© 2020
LECTOR HOUSE LLP

LECTOR HOUSE LLP
E-MAIL: lectorpublishing@gmail.com

SPEAKER SERIES, NUMBER 2.

BEADLE'S DIME NATIONAL SPEAKER
EMBODYING GEMS OF ORATORY AND WIT, PARTICULARLY ADAPTED TO AMERICAN SCHOOLS AND FIRESIDES.

BY

VARIOUS

REVISED AND ENLARGED EDITION.

CONTENTS

Page

- INTRODUCTION. x
- THE UNION AND ITS RESULTS. 1
    Edward Everett, July 4th, 1860.
- OUR COUNTRY'S FUTURE. 3
    Edward Everett's Oration at the Webster Statue Inauguration, 1860.
- THE STATESMAN'S LABORS. 5
    Ibid.
- TRUE IMMORTALITY. 7
    Ibid.
- LET THE CHILDLESS WEEP. 9
    Metta Victoria Victor.
- OUR COUNTRY'S GREATEST GLORY. 11
    Bishop Whipple, of Minnesota, 1860.
- THE UNION A HOUSEHOLD. 12
    Ibid.
- INDEPENDENCE BELL. 13
    July 4th, 1776.
- THE SCHOLAR'S DIGNITY. 15
    Hon. George E. Pugh July 5th, 1859.
- THE CYCLES OF PROGRESS. 17
    Ibid.
- A CHRISTMAS CHANT. 19

Alfred Domett.

- STABILITY OF CHRISTIANITY. 21
  Rev. T. H. Stockton, House of Representatives, March 19th, 1860.

- THE TRUE HIGHER LAW. 22
  Ibid.

- THE ONE GREAT NEED. 24
  Ibid.

- THE SHIP AND THE BIRD.. 25
  Owen Meredith.

- TECUMSEH'S SPEECH TO THE CREEK WARRIORS. 27
  Clairborn's Life of Gen. Dale.

- TERRITORIAL EXPANSION.. 29
  Hon. S. S. Cox, House of Representatives, March 19th, 1860.

- MARTHA HOPKINS. 31
  Phœbe Cary.

- THE BASHFUL MAN'S STORY. 33
  Charles Matthews.

- THE MATTER-OF-FACT MAN. 36
  Anon.

- RICH AND POOR.. 37
  Joseph Barber.

- SEEING THE ECLIPSE. 39
  Anon.

- THE BEAUTIES OF THE LAW.. 40

- GE-LANG! GIT UP! 42
  New Orleans Delta.

- THE RATS OF LIFE. 44
  Charles T. Congdon.

- "THE CREOWNIN' GLORY OF THE UNITED STATES.". 46
  Knickerbocker Magazine.

CONTENTS

- THREE FOOLS.................................47
  C. H. Spurgeon.
- WASHINGTON.................................48
  Hon. Thomas S. Bocock, Feb. 22d, 1860.
- THE SAME....................................50
  Ibid
- THE SAME....................................52
  Ibid
- OUR GREAT INHERITANCE......................54
  John J. Crittenden, 1860.
- EULOGIUM ON HENRY CLAY.....................55
  Lincoln, 1852.
- OHIO..57
  Bancroft's Oration at Cleveland, Sept. 10th, 1860.
- OLIVER HAZARD PERRY........................58
  Ibid.
- OUR DOMAIN..................................60
  Ibid.
- SYSTEMS OF BELIEF...........................62
  Rev. W. H. Milburn, 1860.
- THE INDIAN CHIEF............................64
- THE INDEPENDENT FARMER......................66
  W. W. Fosdick.
- MRS. GRAMMAR'S BALL.........................68
  Anon.
- HOW THE MONEY COMES.........................70
- THE FUTURE OF THE FASHIONS..................72
  Punch.
- LOYALTY TO LIBERTY OUR ONLY HOPE............73
  Bishop Whipple, of Minnesota.

- OUR COUNTRY FIRST, LAST, AND ALWAYS. 74
  Ibid.
- BRITISH INFLUENCE. 75
  John Randolph.
- DEFENSE OF THOMAS JEFFERSON.. 76
  Henry Clay.
- NATIONAL HATREDS ARE BARBAROUS. 77
  Rufus Choate.
- MURDER WILL OUT. 79
  Daniel Webster.
- STRIVE FOR THE BEST.. 81
- EARLY RISING.. 82
  John G. Saxe.
- DEEDS OF KINDNESS. 84
- THE GATES OF SLEEP. 85
  Dr. John Henry.
- THE BUGLE. 87
  Tennyson.
- A HOODISH GEM. 88
- PURITY OF THE AMERICAN STRUGGLE. 89
  By Hon. Henry Wilson. 1859.
- OLD AGE.. 90
  Theodore Parker.
- BEAUTIFUL, AND AS TRUE AS BEAUTIFUL.. 92
- THE DELUGE. 93
- THE WORM OF THE STILL. 95
- MAN'S CONNECTION WITH THE INFINITE. 97
- THE LANGUAGE OF THE EAGLE.. 99

CONTENTS ix

- WASHINGTON. 101
    S. S. Cox.

- AMERICA vs. ENGLAND. 103
    David Dudley Field.

- IF WE KNEW.. 105
    By Ruth Benton.

INTRODUCTION.

It is with real pleasure that this second number of the "Dime Speaker" is given to the public. The issue of the first number has been followed with such a demand as to render this additional volume quite necessary to meet the calls of teachers, students, and others. The experiment of "giving a dollar book for ten cents," which should embrace *more* new and *adaptable* pieces for reading and rehearsal—in prose and poetry, serious and humorous—than any single work yet offered, has, it is needless to say, proven a success in every respect; and this second number of our DIME SPEAKER is given to teachers and scholars in the full assurance of its meeting with their approbation in all respects. It will be found to include some unusually valuable and beautiful pieces for the school-stage, both in prose and verse—most of the matter being from speeches and contributions lately given to the world by the best of our living orators and writers. The effort has been to give as great variety as possible—to suit all tastes and capacities, from the child to the man. It is the purpose of the publishers to continue the series in yearly issues, thus to place in the hands of the youth of our land, at the smallest possible price, books which can not fail to expand their tastes for what is best in style and sentiment, while they shall also offer instruction and amusement, as well to the home circle as to the school-room and exhibition.

BEADLE'S DIME SPEAKER, NO. 2.

THE UNION AND ITS RESULTS.
Edward Everett, July 4th, 1860.

Merely to fill up the wilderness with a population provided with the ordinary institutions and carrying on the customary pursuits of civilized life—though surely no mean achievement—was, by no means, the whole of the work allotted to the United States, and thus far performed with signal activity, intelligence, and success. The founders of America and their descendants have accomplished more and better things. On the basis of a rapid geographical extension, and with the force of teeming numbers, they have, in the very infancy of their political existence, successfully aimed at higher progress in a generous civilization. The mechanical arts have been cultivated with unusual aptitude. Agriculture, manufactures, commerce, navigation, whether by sails or by steam, and the art of printing in all its forms, have been pursued with surprising skill. Great improvements have been made in all those branches of industry, and in the machinery pertaining to them, which have been eagerly adopted in Europe. A more adequate provision has been made for popular education than in almost any other country. There are more seminaries in the United States, where a respectable academical education may be obtained—more, I still mean, in proportion to the population—than in any other country except Germany. The fine arts have reached a high degree of excellence. The taste for music is rapidly spreading in town and country; and every year witnesses productions from the pencil and the chisel of American sculptors and painters, which would adorn any gallery in the world. Our Astronomers, Mathematicians, Naturalists, Chemists, Engineers, Jurists, Publicists, Historians, Poets, Novelists, and Lexicographers, have placed themselves on a level with those of the elder world. The best dictionaries of the English language since Johnson, are those published in America. Our constitutions, whether of the United States or of the separate States, exclude all public provision for the maintenance of religion, but in no part of Christendom is it more generously supported. Sacred science is pursued as diligently and the pulpit commands as high a degree of respect in the United States, as in those countries where the Church is publicly endowed; while the American Missionary operations have won the admiration of the civilized world. Nowhere, I am persuaded, are there more liberal contributions to public-spirited and charitable objects. In a word, there is no branch of the mechanical or fine arts, no department of science, exact or applied, no form of polite literature, no description of social improvement, in which, due allowance being made for the means and resources at command, the progress of the United States has not been satisfactory, and in some respects astonishing.

At this moment the rivers and seas of the globe are navigated with that marvelous application of steam as a propelling power, which was first effected by Fulton. The harvests of the civilized world are gathered by American reapers; the newspapers which lead the journalism of Europe are printed on American presses; there are railroads in Europe constructed by American engineers and traveled by American locomotives; troops armed with American weapons, and ships of war built in American dockyards. In the factories of Europe there is machinery of American invention or improvement; in their observatories telescopes of American construction, and apparatus of American invention for recording the celestial phenomena. America contests with Europe the introduction into actual use of the electric telegraph, and her mode of operating it is adopted throughout the French empire. American authors in almost every department are found on the shelves of European libraries. It is true no American Homer, Virgil, Dante, Copernicus, Shakspeare, Bacon, Milton, Newton, has risen on the world. These mighty geniuses seem to be exceptions in the history of the human mind. Favorable circumstances do not produce them, nor does the absence of favorable circumstances prevent their appearance. Homer rose in the dawn of Grecian culture; Virgil flourished in the court of Augustus; Dante ushered in the birth of the new European civilization; Copernicus was reared in a Polish cloister; Shakspeare was trained in the greenroom of the theater; Milton was formed while the elements of English thought and life were fermenting toward a great political and moral revolution; Newton under the profligacy of the Restoration. Ages may elapse before any country will produce a man like these, as two centuries have passed since the last-mentioned of them was born. But if it is really a matter of reproach to the United States that, in the comparatively short period of their existence as a people, they have not added another name to this illustrious list (which is equally true of all the other nations of the earth), they may proudly boast of one example of life and character, one career of disinterested service, one model, of public virtue, one type of human excellence, of which all the countries and all the ages may be searched in vain for the parallel. I need not—on this day I need not—speak the peerless name. It is stamped on your hearts, it glistens in your eyes, it is written on every page of your history, on the battle-fields of the Revolution, on the monuments of your fathers, on the portals of your capitols. It is heard in every breeze that whispers over the fields of Independent America. And he was all our own. He grew up on the soil of America; he was nurtured at her bosom. She loved and trusted him in his youth; she honored and revered him in his age; and, though she did not wait for death to canonize his name, his precious memory, with each succeeding year, has sunk more deeply into the hearts of his countrymen.

OUR COUNTRY'S FUTURE.

Edward Everett's Oration at the Webster Statue Inauguration, 1860.

What else is there, in the material system of the world, so wonderful as this concealment of the Western Hemisphere for ages behind the mighty vail of waters? How could such a secret be kept from the foundation of the world till the end of the fifteenth century? What so astonishing as the concurrence, within less than a century, of the invention of printing, the demonstration of the true system of the heavens, and this great world-discovery? What so mysterious as the dissociation of the native tribes of this continent from the civilized and civilizable races of man? What so remarkable, in political history, as the operation of the influences, now in conflict, now in harmony, under which the various nations of the old world sent their children to occupy the new; great populations silently stealing into existence; the wilderness of one century swarming in the next with millions; ascending the streams, crossing the mountains, struggling with a wild hard nature, with savage foes, with rival settlements of foreign powers, but ever onward, onward? What so propitious as this long colonial training in the school of chartered government? and then, when the fullness of time had come, what so majestic, amidst all its vicissitudes and all its trials, as the Grand Separation—mutually beneficial in its final results to both parties—the dread appeal to arms, that venerable Continental Congress, the august Declaration, the strange alliance of the oldest monarchy of Europe with the Infant Republic? And, lastly, what so worthy the admiration of men and angels as the appearance of him the expected—him the Hero—raised up to conduct the momentous conflict to its auspicious issue in the Confederation, the Union, the Constitution?

Is this a theme not unworthy of the pen and the mind of Webster? Then consider the growth of the country, thus politically ushered into existence and organized under that Constitution, as delineated in his address on the laying the corner-stone of the extension of the Capitol—the thirteen colonies that accomplished the Revolution multiplied to thirty-two independent States, a single one of them exceeding in population the old thirteen; the narrow border of settlement along the coast, fenced in by France and the native tribes, expanded to the dimensions of the continent; Louisiana, Florida, Texas, New Mexico, California, Oregon—territories equal to the great monarchies of Europe—added to the Union; and the two millions of population which fired the imagination of Burke, swelled to twenty-four millions, during the lifetime of Mr. Webster, and in seven short years, which have since elapsed, increased to thirty!

With these stupendous results in his own time as the unit of calculation;

beholding under Providence with each decade of years, a new people, millions strong, emigrants in part from the Old World, but mainly bone of our bone, and flesh of our flesh, the children of the soil, growing up to inhabit the waste places of the continent, to inherit and transmit the rights and blessings which we have received from our fathers; recognizing in the Constitution and in the Union established by it the creative influence which, as far as human agencies go, has wrought these miracles of growth and progress, and which wraps up in sacred reserve the expansive energy with which the work is to be carried on and perfected, he looked forward with patriotic aspiration to the time, when, beneath its ægis, the whole wealth of our civilization would be poured out, not only to fill up the broad interstices of settlement, if I may so express myself, in the old thirteen and their young and thriving sister States, already organized in the West, but, in the lapse of time, to found a hundred new republics in the valley of the Missouri and beyond the Rocky Mountains, till our letters and our arts, our schools and our churches, our laws and our liberties, shall be carried from the arctic circle to the tropics, "from the rising of the sun to the going down thereof."

THE STATESMAN'S LABORS.
Ibid.

This prophetic glance, not merely at the impending, but the distant future, this reliance on the fulfillment of the great design of Providence, illustrated through our whole history, to lavish upon the people of this country the accumulated blessings of all former stages of human progress, made Webster more tolerant of the tardy and irregular advances and temporary wanderings from the path of what he deemed a wise and sound policy, than those fervid spirits, who dwell exclusively in the present, and make less allowance for the gradual operation of moral influences. This was the case in reference to the great sectional controversy, which now so sharply divides and so violently agitates the country. He not only confidently anticipated, what the lapse of seven years since his decease has witnessed and is witnessing, that the newly acquired and the newly organized territories of the Union would grow up into free States; but in common with all or nearly all the statesmen of the last generation, he believed that free labor would ultimately prevail throughout the country. He thought he saw that, in the operation of the same causes which have produced this result in the Middle and Eastern States, it was visibly taking place in the States north of the cotton-growing region; and he inclined to the opinion that there also, under the influence of physical and economical causes, free labor would eventually be found more productive, and would therefore be ultimately established.

For these reasons, bearing in mind, what all admit, that the complete solution of the mighty problem, which now so greatly tasks the prudence and patriotism of the wisest and best in the land, is beyond the delegated powers of the general government; that it depends, as far as the States are concerned, on their independent legislation, and that it is of all others a subject, in reference to which public opinion and public sentiment will most powerfully influence the law; that much in the lapse of time, without law, is likely to be brought about by degrees, and gradually done and permitted, as in Missouri, at the present day, while nothing is to be hoped from external interference, whether of exhortation or rebuke; that in all human affairs controlled by self-governing communities extreme opinions and extreme courses, on the one hand, generally lead to extreme opinions and extreme courses on the other; and that nothing will more contribute to the earliest practicable relief of the country from this most prolific source of conflict and estrangement, than to prevent its being introduced into our party organizations, he deprecated its being allowed to find a place among the political issues of the day, north or south, and seeking a platform on which honest and patriotic men might meet and stand, he thought he had found it, where our fathers did, in the Constitution.

It is true that, in interpreting the fundamental law on this subject, a diversity of opinion between the two sections of the Union presents itself. This has ever been the case, first or last, in relation to every great question which has divided the country. It is the unfailing incident of constitutions, written or unwritten; an evil to be dealt with in good faith, by prudent and enlightened men, in both sections of the Union, seeking, as Washington sought, the public good, and giving expression to the patriotic common-sense of the people.

Such, I have reason to believe, were the principles entertained by Mr. Webster; not certainly those best calculated to win a temporary popularity in any part of the Union, in times of passionate sectional agitation which, between the extremes of opinion, leaves no middle ground for moderate counsels. If any one could have found and could have trodden such ground with success, he would seem to have been qualified to do it, by his transcendent talent, his mature experience, his approved temper and calmness, and his tried patriotism. If he failed of finding such a path for himself or the country—while we thoughtfully await what time and an all-wise Providence has in store for ourselves and our children—let us remember that his attempt was the highest and the purest which can engage the thoughts of a Statesman and a Patriot: peace on earth, good-will toward men, harmony and brotherly love among the children of our common country.

TRUE IMMORTALITY.
Ibid.

It has been the custom, from the remotest antiquity, to preserve and to hand down to posterity, in bronze and in marble, the counterfeit presentment of illustrious men.

Your long rows of quarried granite may crumble to the dust; the cornfields in yonder villages, ripening to the sickle, may, like the plains of stricken Lombardy, a short time ago, be kneaded into bloody clods, by the maddening wheels of artillery; this populous city, like the old cities of Etruria and the Campagna Romana, may be desolated by the pestilence which walketh in darkness, may decay with the lapse of time, and the busy mart, which now rings with the joyous din of trade, become as lonely and still as Carthage or Tyre, as Babylon and Nineveh, but the names of the great and good shall survive the desolation and the ruin; the memory of the wise, the brave, the patriotic, shall never perish. Yes, Sparta is a wheat field; a Bavarian prince holds court at the foot of the Acropolis; the traveling virtuoso digs for marbles in the Roman Forum and beneath the ruins of the Temple of Jupiter Capitolinus; but Lycurgus and Leonidas, and Miltiades and Demosthenes, and Cato and Tully "still live;" and Webster still lives, and all the great and good shall live in the heart of ages, while marble and bronze shall endure; and when marble and bronze have perished, they shall "still live" in memory so long as men shall reverence Law, and honor Patriotism, and love Liberty!

That solemn event, which terminates the material existence, becomes by the sober revisions of contemporary judgment, aided by offices of respectful and affectionate commemoration, the commencement of a nobler life on earth. The wakeful eyes are closed, the feverish pulse is still, the tired and trembling limbs are relieved from their labors, and the aching head is laid to rest on the lap of its mother earth, like a play-worn child at the close of a summer's day; but all that we honored and loved in the living man begins to live again in a new and higher being of influence and fame. It was given but to a limited number to listen to the living voice of Daniel Webster, and they can never listen to it again; but the wise teachings, the grave admonitions, the patriotic exhortations which fell from his tongue will be gathered together and garnered up in the memory of millions. The cares, the toils, the sorrows; the conflicts with others, the conflicts of the fervent spirit with itself; the sad accidents of humanity, the fears of the brave, the follies of the wise, the errors of the learned; all that dashed the cup of enjoyment with bitter drops and strewed sorrowful ashes over the beauty of expectation and promise; the treacherous friend, the ungenerous rival, the mean and malignant foe; the uncharitable prejudice which withheld the just tribute of praise, the human frailty which wove sharp thorns into the wreath of solid merit—all these in ordinary cases are buried in the grave of the illustrious dead; while their brilliant talents, their deeds of benevolence and public spirit, their wise and eloquent words, their healing counsels, their generous affections, the whole man, in short, whom we revered and loved and would fain imitate, especially when his image is impressed upon our recollections by the pencil or the chisel, goes forth to the admiration of the latest posterity. *Extinctus amabitur idem.*

LET THE CHILDLESS WEEP.
Metta Victoria Victor.

The news is flying along the streets:
It leaves a smile with each face it meets.
The heart of London is all on fire—
Its throbbing veins beat faster and higher—
With eager triumph they beat so fast—
"The Malakoff—Malakoff falls at last!"
Hark to the murmur, the shout, the yell—
"The Malakoff's fallen!"—well, 'tis well!
But let the childless weep.

I am faint and stunn'd by the crowd;
My head aches with the tumult loud.
On this step I will sit me down,
Where the city palaces o'er me frown.
I would these happy people could see
Sights which are never absent from me;
The sound of their joy to sobs might swell,
They would swallow tears—well—it is well!
But let the childless weep.

If they could see my two young sons
Shatter'd and torn by Russian guns,—
The only children God gave me—dead!
With the rough earth for a dying bed.
Side by side, in the trenches deep—
Perchance they would weep as I must weep.
No sons of theirs on that red hill fell,
And so they smile and say, "'tis well!"
But let the childless weep.

I know where in the cottages low
Women's faces grow white with woe;
Where throats are choked with tears unshed
When widows' children ask for bread.
I think of one whose heart has grown
As cold and heavy as this stone.
But cabinets never think so low
As a mother's anguish, and so—and so

Why let the childless weep.

O Queen! your children around you sleep;
Their rest at night is sweet and deep.
Do you ever think of the mothers many
Whose sons you required, and left not any?
Do you think of young limbs bruised and crush'd
And laughing voices forever hush'd?
My soul with a fierce rage might swell,
But grief hath all the place—'tis well!
Let the childless weep.

Could God have seen with prophet eye,
When He piled the Malakoff hill so high,
That it was to be soaked through and through
With streams and streams of blood-red dew,
And covered over with anguish?—no!
Or He would have leveled it small and low.
It is man who is haughty, fierce, and cruel—
Who heaps on his altar the living fuel!
Let the childless weep.

England! England! haughty and bold!
You still covet what you behold;
To have your own proud will and way
You will make widows, thousands a day.
You buy your power with human life,
And the sobbing child and hopeless wife
Give up their dearest at your call—
But hearts must break and towers must fall
Let the childless weep.

Weep? I can not weep while around
Swells the victory's awful sound.
The Malakoff fell,—but England's way
O'er the bosoms that loved her deepest lay.
Victoria's children laugh in glee!—
Does she remember mine, or me?
Oh, footman, leave me this cold stone—
My sons are dead and I am alone—
The childless can not weep.

OUR COUNTRY'S GREATEST GLORY.
Bishop Whipple, of Minnesota, 1860.

The true glory of a nation is in an intelligent, honest, industrious Christian people. The civilization of a nation depends on their individual character; a constitution which is not the outgrowth of this is not worth the parchment on which it is written. You look in vain in the past for a single instance where the people have preserved their liberties after their individual character was lost. The ruler represents the people, and laws and institutions are the simple outgrowth of domestic character. It is not in the magnificence of the home of the ruler, not in the beautiful creations of art lavished on public edifices, not in costly cabinets of pictures or public libraries, not in proud monuments of achievements in battle, not in the number or wealth of its cities, that we find pledges of national glory. The ruler may gather around his palace the treasures of the world, amid a brutalized people; the senate chamber may retain its faultless proportions long after the voice of patriotism is hushed within its walls; the marble may commemorate a glory which has forever departed. Art and letters may bring no lesson to a people whose heart is dead; the only glory of a nation is in the living temple of a loyal, industrious, and upright people. The busy click of machinery, the merry ring of the anvil, the lowing of peaceful herds, and the song of the harvest home, are sweeter music than pæans of departed glory or songs of triumph in war. The vine-clad cottage of the hill-side, the cabin of the woodsman, and the rural home of the farmer are the true citadels of any country. There is a dignity in honest toil which belongs not to the display of wealth or the luxury of fashion. The man who drives the plow, or swings his ax in the forest, or with cunning fingers plies the tools of his craft, is as truly the servant of his country, as the statesman in the senate or the soldier in battle. The safety of a nation depends not on the wisdom of its statesmen or the bravery of its generals; the tongue of eloquence never saved a nation tottering to its fall; the sword of a warrior never stayed its destruction. There is a surer defense in every Christian home. I say Christian home, for I know of no glory to manhood which comes not from the cross. I know of no rights wrung from tyranny, no truth rescued from darkness and bigotry, which has not waited on a Christian civilization. Would you see the image of true glory, I would show you villages where the crown and glory of the people was in purity of character, where the children were gathered in Christian schools, where the voice of prayer goes heavenward, where the people have that most priceless gift—*faith in God*. With this as the basis, and leavened as it will be with brotherly love, there will be no danger in grappling with any evils which exist in our midst; we shall feel that we may work and bide our time, and die knowing that God will bring the victory.

THE UNION A HOUSEHOLD.
Ibid.

The great object which the statesmen of the Revolution sought, was the defense, protection, and good government of the whole, without injustice to any portion of the people. Experience had taught them that it was impossible for a great republic to grow up where its every act of public policy was liable to be thwarted by the vote of the individual States; therefore they framed an organic law at the foundation of our common government, which gave the men of Carolina and Massachusetts a name dearer than any sectional name—the name of an *American citizen*! In that conflict of opinions, by a temper of conciliation and brotherly love, by an earnest loyalty to freedom and profoundest reverence for law, they framed that constitution which has been the admiration of the world.

I yield to no man in my admiration for those noble men whose names are our household words; but in this history I see the hand of God and acknowledge that our nationality was his gift and not the fruits of our fathers' wisdom. Ours is not the only nation who have sought to be free. Strong arms and stout hearts have often failed—the world is filled with the lamentations of the patriots and dirges for the dead. God always gives to a nation its birthright and its name. A nation is not a mere aggregate of households, or villages, or States—national life is something beyond the fact that individual men have banded together for mutual defense. This belonged to the savage tribes who once roamed over this goodly land. They may be strong, daring, freedom-loving men, without national life. There never was a nobler race than the people who dwelt in the fastnesses of Scotland, but their tie was only one of kindred; the family became a clan, separate clans warred with each other in murderous strife, and Scotland was a field of blood. Until the cross was firmly planted in Britain, England had no nationality—it was a land of faction until the law and providence of God became the people's guide, and then the nobler name of Saxon became a Christian name to tell of all that is manly and true. Our national life is the gift of God. No other hand could gather out of other lands millions of people of different tongues and kindred, and mold these into one mighty nation that shall receive into itself the men of every clime, and stamp on them its own mark of individuality, teaching them its language, making them its kin, and binding them as one household under its own constitution and laws.

INDEPENDENCE BELL.

July 4th, 1776.

When it was certain that the Declaration would be adopted and confirmed by the signatures of the delegates in Congress, it was determined to announce the event by ringing the old State-House bell which bore the inscription, "Proclaim liberty to the land: to all the inhabitants thereof!" and the old bellman posted his little boy at the door of the hall to await the instruction of the doorkeeper when to ring. At the word, the little patriot-scion rushed out, and, flinging up his hands, shouted "*Ring!* Ring! RING!"

There was tumult in the city,
In the quaint old Quaker's town,
And the streets were rife with people
Pacing restless up and down;
People gathering at corners,
Where they whisper'd each to each,
And the sweat stood on their temples,
With the earnestness of speech.

As the bleak Atlantic currents
Lash the wild Newfoundland shore,
So they beat against the State-House,
So they surged against the door;
And the mingling of their voices
Made a harmony profound,
'Till the quiet street of chestnuts
Was all turbulent with sound.

"Will they do it?" "Dare they do it?"
"Who is speaking?" "What's the news?"
"What of Adams?" "What of Sherman?"
"Oh, God grant they won't refuse!"
"Make some way there!" "Let me nearer!"
"I am stifling!" "Stifle, then!
When a nation's life's at hazard,
We've no time to think of men!"

So they beat against the portal,
Man and woman, maid and child;
And the July sun in heaven

On the scene look'd down and smiled,
The same sun that saw the Spartan
Shed his patriot-blood in vain,
Now beheld the soul of freedom
All unconquer'd rise again.

See! See! The dense crowd quivers
Through all its lengthy line,
As the boy beside the portal
Looks forth to give the sign!
With his small hands upward lifted,
Breezes dallying with his hair,
Hark! with deep, clear intonation,
Breaks his young voice on the air.

Hush'd the people's swelling murmur,
List the boy's strong joyous cry!
"*Ring!*" he shouts, "Ring! *Grandpa
Ring! Oh*, Ring for *Liberty!*"
And straightway, at the signal,
The old bellman lifts his hand,
And sends the good news, making
Iron-music through the land.

How they shouted! What rejoicing!
How the old bell shook the air,
Till the clang of freedom ruffled
The calm gliding Delaware!
How the bonfires and the torches
Illumed the night's repose,
And from the flames, like Phœnix,
Fair Liberty arose!

That old bell now is silent,
And hush'd its iron tongue,
But the spirit it awaken'd
Still lives,—forever young.
And while we greet the sunlight,
On the fourth of each July,
We'll ne'er forget the bellman,
Who, twixt the earth and sky,
Rung out Our Independence;
Which, please God, *shall never die*!

THE SCHOLAR'S DIGNITY.
Hon. George E. Pugh July 5th, 1859.

The purpose of all genuine effort, beyond the satisfaction of physical wants, should be to enlarge the compass of human sympathy and desire, to purify, elevate, ennoble the intellectual constitution of our race. God has so created us that these results can be attained by simple and even direct agencies. Man is a sympathetic being; and the full discharge of his obligation toward his own family, his friends, his neighbors, is the method by which he can best discharge his duty in other relations; toward God and his country, toward the millions of his fellow-beings now alive, and the millions who will inherit the earth in a course of ages. Hence arise man's real pleasures, and (not less) his noblest responsibilities and actions. But, as our nature is composed of appetites and passions which rightly adjusted, each with another, lift us almost to the dignity of the Godhead, but when disorganized, show us to be meaner than the brutes; so civil society, or the association of mankind pursuant to the Divine order, while capable, in its normal state, of the utmost happiness for all its members, is now disorganized and demoralized, its sweet bells of sympathy turned to discord, even its charities stained by selfishness and base pretension; its capacities for good entirely perverted to the oppression, to the cruel debasements of the multitude, and to the unjust advantage of a few. Here is the field of chivalry for him—scholar and squire who would be something more—conscious of his earnest duty, of the vast rewards which must crown success, and alive to the inspiration of all the past, the present, and the future; here is a field on which he may win the gilded spurs of knighthood, and where, with his own arm, he can truly redress the innocent, rescue the unfortunate, and reclaim even the oppressor to a recognition of the rights of the oppressed. Or, if he would choose a holier part, although less conspicuous, it may be, let him join that valiant array of pioneers which is marching now (as, in time past, it ever has marched) at the head of the generation; hewing down primeval forests of ignorance; bridging the torrents of crime; leveling mountains of doubt and difficulty; filling up quagmires of sorrow; that so, in age after age, the hosts of pilgrims from the cradle to the grave shall traverse their distance without harm, and measurably anticipate, if not realize, the beatitude of toil forever accomplished.

In a true sense, the scholar is a king of the noblest power. Not his that dominion which exercises itself over the bodies of men, subduing alike their happiness and their will, making of his fellow-creatures a mere sport or convenience, but that dominion which exists by the full consent of the governed, and without which, in reality, their happiness and peace can not be secured. [Nam, uti genus hominum compositum ex anima et corpore, ita res cunctæ, studiaque omnia nostra, corporis alia, alia animi naturam sequuntur. Igitur, præclara facies, magnæ divitiæ, ad hoc vis corporis, alia hujuscemodi, omnia brevi dilabuntur; at ingenii egregia facinora, sicuti anima, immortalia sunt. Postremo, corporis et fortunæ bonorum, ut initium, finis est: omnia orta occidunt, et aucta senescunt: animus incorruptus, æternus, RECTOR HUMANI GENERIS, agit atque habet cuncta, neque ipse habetur.] The liberty of men does not stand in rebellion against the truth, nor against the truly-anointed genius of the age:

> Unjustly thou depravest it with the name
> Of servitude, to serve whom God ordains,
> Or Nature; God and Nature bid the same,
> When he who rules is worthiest, and excels
> Them whom he governs. This is servitude,
> To serve th' unwise, or him who hath rebell'd
> Against his worthier.

THE CYCLES OF PROGRESS.
Ibid.

The world moves in a grand cycle of days, and weeks, and months, and years, susceptible of approximation, but not of exact ascertainment. There are cycles, also, of the human understanding; or, at least, of opinions with regard to the faculties and organism of the human intellect. Locke was thought to have demonstrated, by unanswerable argument, our entire lack of innate ideas; thus demolishing the foundation upon which others had erected so many and such various theories. But now Kant has proven, by a logic far more subtle, and altogether more conclusive, that the mind acts only in certain processes, or by means of certain categories, which are the laws of its organization, and whence result conceptions or ideas not derived from experience, or observation, or confidence in others. Plato arrived at the same conclusion two thousand years ago, although he supposed these conceptions or ideas to be the *reminiscences* of a former and superior state of intellectual existence. What has Kant accomplished, in all his philosophy, except our remission to the speculations of Plato, as enforced and illustrated by the wisdom of revealed religion? And so, in the world of moral sentiment, there must be cycles of repetition and restoration, but of restoration with *new auspices*, and informed by principles of higher and pure significance.

The Age of Chivalry was an age of moral improvement, an age of sympathy and generous enterprise, after centuries of darkness, antagonism, and oppression. When scholars, therefore, shall have become true to themselves, true to the mission of their faith and labors, as against the overwhelming allurement of our time; shall have become the actual prophets, and priests, and rulers, which once they were, another Age of Chivalry will arise and dawn upon earth. It will restore us a Government paternal in character, and yet stripped of the usurpations by which government is now rendered oppressive; it will restore us a Church of pristine authority and influence, but authority and influence derived from purity in practice as well as in precept. And with these two elements so long extinct or lost—leaving mankind to all the terrors of tyranny and all the wiles of imposture—with a Church and a Government reflecting the Divine conception of men's duties toward their Creator and toward each other, will Human Society attain, at last, the summit of human perfection. Then will the original brotherhood and equality of our race be forever acknowledged; then will there be work for all, and wages for work, instead of the injustice, the crime, the misery, the wasteful disorder which fill our hearts with so much despondency and woe. This Chivalry is of magnificent design; since to the faith, to the hope, to the steadfastness of our fathers, to their moral excellence and solid greatness, will thus be united the wondrous material achievements for which we have been so distinguished—a Chivalry of splendors enhanced as well as rekindled, or splendors essentially bright, and joyous, and immortal.

History tells us of republics full of promise and full of glory like our own. Such were those which clustered upon the shores of the Mediterranean, in almost the same latitude with us, and accomplished, centuries ago, their rise, their zenith, and their fall. Such were those free states and cities which braved the bleakness and inclemency of the Baltic and German coasts; and which likewise had their increase, and fullness, and extinction. These were all the children of Commerce, and followed her along the borders of the sea. Their ships explored the very ends of the world; laid the Indies under tribute; and on this remote continent, also, planted colonies and outposts of civilization. Alas! those republics and free states and cities have gone to their decay; the armed legions of Despotism tread upon their tombs, and scatter even their sacred ashes to the winds. But may our New World, which inherits their enterprise as well as their liberty, rejuvenate the nations grown old in oppression and despair, and plant upon the Eastern Continent the germs of a Civilization nobler than has yet been recognized—nobler than was ever sung by the poets, or foretold by oracles—a Civilization which shall raise up LABOR from its fallen estate, heal its infirmities, cover its nakedness, and enthrone it with honor; as the rescued maniac, by Divine compassion, was seated near the feet of our Saviour, clothed, and in his right mind!

A CHRISTMAS CHANT.

Alfred Domett.

It was the calm and silent night!
Seven hundred years and fifty-three
Had Rome been growing up to might,
And now was queen of land and sea!
No sound was heard of clashing wars,
Peace brooded o'er the hush'd domain;
Apollo, Pallas, Jove, and Mars,
Held undisturb'd their ancient reign,
In the solemn midnight,
Centuries ago!

'Twas in the calm and silent night!
The senator of haughty Rome
Impatient urged his chariot's flight,
From lordly revel rolling home.
Triumphal arches, gleaming, swell
His breast with thoughts of boundless sway;
What reck'd the Roman what befell
A paltry province far away,
In the solemn midnight,
Centuries ago?

Within that province far away
Went plodding home a weary boor;
A streak of light before him lay,
Fallen through a half-shut stable-door
Across his path. He paused, for naught
Told what was going on within;
How keen the stars, his only thought;
The air, how calm, and cold, and thin,
In the solemn midnight,
Centuries ago!

Oh, strange indifference! low and high
Drowsed over common joys and cares;
The earth was still, but knew not why;
The world was listening—unawares!
How calm a moment may precede

One that shall thrill the world forever!
To that still moment, none would heed,
Man's doom was link'd, no more to sever,
In the solemn midnight,
Centuries ago!

It is the calm and silent night!
A thousand bells ring out, and throw
Their joyous peals abroad, and smite
The darkness, charm'd and holy now;
The night that erst no shame had worn,
To it a happy name is given;
For in that stable lay, new-born,
The peaceful Prince of Earth and Heaven,
In the solemn midnight,
Centuries ago!

STABILITY OF CHRISTIANITY.

Rev. T. H. Stockton, House of Representatives, March 19th, 1860.

I contemplate the heaven and earth of the old world: the overrulings of Providence and changes of society there. I think of the passing away of the whole circle of ancient Mediterranean civilization. I think of the dark ages of Europe. I think of the morning of the Reformation, and the fore-gleamings of "the latter-day glory." I think of Art, and her printing-press; of Commerce, and her compass; of Science, and her globe; of Religion, and her Bible. I contemplate the opening of the heaven and earth of the New World: the overrulings of Providence and changes of society here. I think of the passing away of savage simplicities, and of the rude semblances of civilization in Mexico and Peru, and of earlier and later declensions. I think of the gracious reservation of our own inheritance for present and nobler occupancy. I think of our Revolution, and its result of Independence. I think of our first Union, first Congress, first prayer in Congress, and first Congressional order for the Bible; and of our wonderful enlargement, development, and enrichment since. And, in view of all—of the whole heaven and whole earth of the whole world; and of all changes, social and natural, past, present, and future; profoundly and unalterably assured, as I trust we all are, that the truth as it is "in Jesus" is the only stability in the universe—I feel justified, in invoking, this day, your renewal of our common and constant confession—that: Heaven and earth shall pass away, but the words of Christ shall never pass away. And, standing where we do, on the central summit of this great Confederacy, unequalled in all history for all manner of blessings,—if we did not so confess Christ; if we did not cherish the simple confidence of His primitive disciples, and hail the coming of our Lord with hosannas; if we could ignobly hold our peace,—the very statues of the Capitol "would immediately cry out;" the marble lips of Columbus, Penn, and Washington, of War and Peace, of the Pioneer, and of Freedom, would part to praise His name; and the stones of the foundation and walls, of the arcades and corridors, of the rotunda and halls, would respond to their glad and grand acclaim.

From Maine to Florida, from Florida to Texas, from Texas to California, from California to Oregon, and from Oregon back to Maine; our lake States, gulf States, and ocean States; our river States, prairie States, and mountain States, all unite in confessing and blessing His name, beholding His glory, surrounding His throne, high and lifted up, and ever crying, like the six-winged seraphim, one to another, far and near, from the North and the South, from the East and the West: "Holy, holy, holy is the Lord of hosts, the whole earth is full of His glory!"

THE TRUE HIGHER LAW.
Ibid.

We hear much of the higher law; and the application of the phrase to civil affairs has excited great prejudice and given great offense. But, what is the higher law? It is said to be something higher than the Constitution of the United States. Can there be a law, within these United higher than the Constitution of the United States? If there can be and is such a law—what is it? I need not and will not recite inferior, questionable, and inappropriate answers here. But, is there not one unquestionable answer? Suppose it be said, that, in relation to all subjects to which it was designed to apply, and properly does apply, the Bible is a higher Law than the Constitution of the United States? Will any man, unless an utter infidel, deny this? Surely not. Waiving its practical operations, certainly, as an abstract proposition, this must be admitted as true. It may be extended, so as to include all our State constitutions, and all our Church constitutions, and all our more Social constitutions. Put them all together, magnify and boast of them as we may, not only is the Bible a higher law, but it is an infinitely higher law. For thus saith the Lord: "As the heavens are higher than the earth, so are my ways higher than your ways, and my thoughts than your thoughts." Therefore, also, the universal and perpetual prophetic challenge: "Oh, earth, earth, earth, hear the word of the Lord!"

All human constitutions, social, ecclesiastical, and civil, are changeable, and contain provisions for change; but, the Bible is unchangeable. Instead of any provision for change, it is guarded, at all points, against change. The writer of its first five books declares in the last of the five: "Ye shall not *add* unto the word which I command you, neither shall ye *diminish* from it, that ye may keep the commandments of the Lord your God, which I command you." And, in like manner, the author of its last five books, declares in the last of the five: "If any man shall *add* unto these things, God shall add unto him the plagues that are written in this book: and if any man shall *take away* from the words of the book of this prophecy, God shall take away his part out of the book of life, and out of the holy city, and from the things which are written in this book." And so Isaiah, standing midway between Moses and John, exclaims: "Lift up your eyes to the heavens, and look upon the earth beneath; for the heavens shall vanish away like smoke, and the earth shall wax old like a garment, and they that dwell therein shall die in like manner; but My salvation shall be forever, and My righteousness shall not be abolished." Therefore, it is only in accordance with the testimony of all His witnesses, that Christ Himself avers: "Think not that I am come to destroy the law, or the prophets: I am not come to destroy, but to fulfill. For verily I say unto you, Till heaven and earth pass, one jot or one tittle shall in no wise pass from the law, till all be fulfilled. Heaven and earth shall pass away, but My words shall not pass away."

THE ONE GREAT NEED.
Ibid.

Tell me, oh, tell me, what is it we need? Do we need health, or genius, or learning, or eloquence, or pleasure, or fame, or power? Do we need wealth, or rank, or office? Does any one of us need to be chaplain, or clerk, or representative, or senator, or speaker, or vice-president? an officer of the army or navy? a member or head of any department? a foreign minister? a cabinet officer? or even a successor in the line of presidents of the United States? Is such our need? Ah, no! we need salvation.

What did I say in the beginning? Did I not say we need elevation? as men, Americans, and Christians, we need elevation: in our persons and families, states and churches, we need elevation. Certainly I did thus speak, and meant all I said.

Oh, my Friends! All the distinctions alluded to such as we know them here, are comparatively little things. Greater things are in prospect; but these things, though they seem great, are really little. Pause, think, recall what life has taught you—what observation and experience have combined to impress most deeply upon your consciousness—and begin your review with the sad words, *after all*! After all, health is a little thing, and genius is a little thing, and learning, and eloquence, and pleasure, and fame, and power, and wealth, and rank, and office, all earthly things are little things. How little satisfaction they yield while they last, and how soon they pass away!

THE SHIP AND THE BIRD.
Owen Meredith.

Hear a song that was born in the land of my birth!
The anchors are lifted, the fair ship is free,
And the shout of the mariners floats in its mirth
'Twixt the light in the sky and the light on the sea.

And this ship is a world. She is freighted with souls,
She is freighted with merchandise; proudly she sails
With the Labor that stores, and the Will that controls
The gold in the ingots, the silk in the bales.

From the gardens of Pleasure, where reddens the rose,
And the scent of the cedar is faint on the air,
Past the harbors of Traffic, sublimely she goes,
Man's hopes o'er the world of the waters to bear!

Where the cheer from the harbors of Traffic is heard,
Where the gardens of Pleasure fade fast on the sight,
O'er the rose, o'er the cedar, there passes a bird;
'Tis the Paradise Bird, never known to alight.

And that bird, bright and bold as a poet's desire,
Roams her own native heavens, the realms of her birth,
There she soars like a seraph, she shines like a fire,
And her plumage hath never been sullied by earth.

And the mariners greet her; there's song on each lip,
For the bird of good omen, and joy in each eye,
And the ship and the bird, and the bird and the ship,
Together go forth over ocean and sky.

Fast, fast fades the land! far the rose-gardens flee,
And far fleet the harbors. In regions unknown
The ship is alone on a desert of sea,
And the bird in a desert of sky is alone.

In those regions unknown, o'er that desert of air,
Down that desert of waters—tremendous in wrath—
The storm-wind Euroclydon leaps from his lair,
And cleaves through the waves of the ocean, his path.

And the bird in the cloud, and the ship on the wave.

Overtaken, are beaten about by wild gales,
And the mariners all rush their cargo to save,
Of the gold in the ingots, the silk in the bales.

Lo! a wonder which never before hath been heard
For it never before hath been given to sight;
On the ship hath descended the Paradise Bird,
The Paradise Bird never known to alight!

The bird which the mariners bless'd, when each lip
Had a song for the omen which gladden'd each eye,
The bright bird for shelter hath flown to the ship
From the wrath on the sea and the wrath in the sky.

But the mariners heed not the bird any more,
They are felling the masts—they are furling the sails,
Some are working, some weeping, and some wrangling o'er
Their gold in the ingots, their silk in the bales.

Souls of men are on board; wealth of man in the hold;
And the storm-wind Euroclydon sweeps to his prey;
And who heeds the bird? "Save the silk and the gold!"
And the bird from her shelter the gust sweeps away!

Poor Paradise Bird! on her lone flight once more
Back again in the wake of the wind she is driven—
To be whelm'd in the storm, or above it to soar,
And, if rescued from ocean, to vanish in heaven!

And the ship rides the waters, and weathers the gales:
From the haven she nears the rejoicing is heard.
All hands are at work on the ingots, the bales,
Save a child, sitting lonely, who misses—the Bird!

TECUMSEH'S SPEECH TO THE CREEK WARRIORS

Clairborn's Life of Gen. Dale.

In defiance of the white warriors of Ohio and Kentucky, I have traveled through their settlements, once our favorite hunting-grounds. No war-whoop was sounded, but there is blood on our knives. The pale faces felt the blow, but knew not whence it came.

Accursed be the race that has seized on our country and made women of our warriors. Our fathers, from their tombs, reproach us as slaves and cowards. I hear them now in the wailing winds.

The Muscogee was once a mighty people. The Georgians trembled at our war-whoop, and the maidens of my tribe, in the distant lakes, sung the prowess of your warriors, and sighed for their embraces.

Now, your very blood is white, your tomahawks have no edge, your bows and arrows were buried with your fathers. O Muscogees! brethren of my mother, brush from your eyelids the sleep of slavery; once more strike for vengeance—once more for your country! The spirits of the mighty dead complain. The tears drop from the weeping skies. Let the white race perish!

They seize your land; they corrupt your women; they trample on the ashes of your dead!

Back whence they came, upon a trail of blood, they must be driven.

Back! back, ay, into the great water whose accursed waves brought them to our shore!

Burn their dwellings! Destroy their stock! Slay their wives and children! The red man owns the country, and the pale face must never enjoy it!

War now! War forever! War upon the living! War upon the dead! Dig their very corpses from the grave. Our country must give no rest to a white man's bones.

All the tribes of the North are dancing the war dance. Two mighty warriors across the seas will send us arms.

Tecumseh will soon return to his country. My prophets shall tarry with you. They will stand between you and the bullets of your enemies. When the white man approaches you, the yawning earth shall swallow him up.

Soon shall you see my arm of fire stretched athwart the sky. I will stamp my foot at Tippecanoe, and the very earth shall shake.

TERRITORIAL EXPANSION.

Hon. S. S. Cox, House of Representatives, March 19th, 1860.

Is there any American who wishes to consult European Powers as to the propriety or policy of our territorial expansion? Is there any one who fears a fatal blow from these Powers? We do not exist by the sufferance of Europe, but by its insufferance. We did not grow to our present greatness by its fostering care, but by its neglect, and in spite of its malevolence. We do not ask its pardon for being born, nor need we apologize to it for growing. It has endeavored to prevent even the legitimate extension of our commerce, and to confine us to our own continent. But if we can buy Cuba of Spain, it is our business with Spain. If we have to take it, it is our business with Providence. If we must save Mexico, and make its weakness our strength, we have no account to render unto Europe or its dynasties.

If European Powers choose to expand their empire and energize their people, we have no protests, no arms to prevent them. England may push from India through the Himalayas to sell her calicoes to the numberless people of Asia, and divide with France the empires of India, Burmah, and China. Civilization does not lose by their expansion. Russia may push her diplomacy upon Pekin, and her armies through the Caucasus, and upon Persia and Tartary; she may even plant her Greek cross again on the mosque of St. Sophia, and take the Grecian Levant into her keeping as the head of its church and civilization. France may plant her forts and arts upon the shores of the Red Sea; complete the canalization of Suez; erect another Carthage on the shores of the Mediterranean; bind her natural limits from Mont Blanc, in Savoy, to Nice, upon the sea. Sardinia may become the nucleus of the Peninsula, and give to Italy a name and a nationality. Even Spain, proud and poor, may fight over again in Africa the romantic wars with the Morescoes, by which she educated that chivalry and adventure, which three centuries ago made her the mistress of the New World. She may demand territory of Morocco, as she has, as indemnity for the war. America has no inquiry to make, no protocol to sign. These are the movements of an active age. They indicate health, not disease—growth, not decay. They are links in the endless chain of Providence. They prove the mutability of the most imperial of human institutions; but, to the philosophic observer, they move by a law as fixed as that which makes the decay of autumn the herald of spring. They obey the same law by which the constellations change their places in the sky. Astronomers tell us that the "southern cross," which guarded the adventurer upon the Spanish main four centuries ago, and which now can be seen, the most beautiful emblem of our salvation, shining down through a Cuban and Mexican night,—just before the Christian era, glittered in our northern heavens! The same GREAT WILL, which knows no North and no South, and which is sending again, by an irreversible law, the southern cross to our northern skies, on its everlasting cycle of emigration—does it not control the revolutions of nations, and the vicissitudes of empires? The very stars in their courses are "Knights of the Golden Circle," and illustrate the record of human advancement. They are the type of that territorial expansion from which this American continent can not be exempted without annihilation. The finger of Providence points to our nation as the guiding star of this progress. Let him who would either dusk its radiancy, or make it the meteor of a moment, cast again with nicer heed our nation's horoscope.

MARTHA HOPKINS.

Phœbe Cary.

From the kitchen, Martha Hopkins, as she stood there making pies,
Southward looks along the turnpike, with her hand above her eyes;
Where along the distant hill-side, her yearning heifer feeds,
And a little grass is growing in a mighty sight of weeds.

All the air is full of noises for there isn't any school,
And boys, with turned-up pantaloons, are wading in the pool;
Blithely frisk unnumber'd chickens, cackling, for they can not laugh,
Where the airy summits brighten, nimbly leaps a little calf.

Gentle eyes of Martha Hopkins! tell me wherefore do ye gaze,
On the ground that's being furrow'd for the planting of the maize?
Tell me wherefore down the valley, ye have traced the turnpike's way
Far beyond the cattle-pasture, and the brick-yard with its clay?

Ah! the dog-wood tree may blossom, and the door-yard grass may shine,
With the tears of amber dropping from the washing on the line,
And the morning's breath of balsam, lightly brush her faded cheek—
Little recketh Martha Hopkins of the tales of spring they speak.

When the summer's burning solstice on the scanty harvest glow'd,
She had watch'd a man on horseback riding down the turnpike road;
Many times she saw him turning, looking backward quite forlorn,
Till amid her tears she lost him in the shadow of the barn.

Ere the supper-time was over, he had pass'd the kiln of brick,
Cross'd the rushing Yellow River, and forded quite a creek,
And his flat-boat load was taken, at the time for pork and beans,
With the traders of the Wabash, to the wharf at New Orleans.

Therefore watches Martha Hopkins—holding in her hand the pans,
When the sound of distant footsteps seems exactly like a man's:
Not a wind the stove-pipe rattles, not a door behind her jars,
But she seems to hear the rattle of his letting down the bars.

Often sees she men on horseback coming down the turnpike rough,
But they came not as John Jackson, she can see it well enough;
Well she knows the sober trotting of the sorrel horse he keeps,
As he jogs along at leisure, with head down like a sheep's.

She would know him 'mid a thousand, by his home-made coat and vest,

By his socks, which were blue woolen, such as farmers wear out West;
By the color of his trowsers, and his saddle which was spread,
By a blanket which was taken for that purpose from the bed.

None like he the yoke of hickory, on the unbroken ox can throw
None amid his father's cornfields use like him the spade and hoe;
And at all the apple-cuttings, few, indeed, the men are seen,
That can dance with him the polka, touch with him the violin.

He has said to Martha Hopkins, and she thinks she hears him now;
For she knows as well as can be, that he meant to keep his vow;
When the buck-eye tree has blossom'd, and your uncle plants his corn,
Shall the bells of Indiana usher in the wedding-morn.

He has invited his relations, bought a Sunday hat and gown,
And he thinks he'll get a carriage, and they'll spend a day in town;
That their love will newly kindle, and what comfort it will give,
To sit down to the first breakfast in the cabin where they'll live.

Tender eyes of Martha Hopkins! what has got you in such scrape,
'Tis a tear that falls to glitter on the ruffle of her cape;
Ah! the eye of love may brighten, to be certain what it sees,
One man looks like another, when half-hidden by the trees.

But her eager eyes rekindle, she forgets the pies and bread,
As she sees a man on horseback, round the corner of the shed,
Now tie on another apron, get the comb and smooth your hair,
'Tis the sorrel horse that gallops, 'tis John Jackson's self that's there.

THE BASHFUL MAN'S STORY.
Charles Matthews.

Among the various good and bad qualities incident to our nature, I am unfortunately that being overstocked with the one called bashfulness; for you most know, I inherit such an extreme susceptibility of shame, that on the smallest subject of confusion, my blood rushes into my cheeks, and I appear a perfect full-blown rose; in short, I am commonly known by the appellation of "The Bashful Man." The consciousness of this unhappy failing, made me formerly avoid that social company, I should otherwise have been ambitious to appear in: till at length becoming possessed of an ample fortune, by the death of a rich old uncle, and vainly supposing that "money makes the man," I was now determined to shake off my natural timidity, and join in the gay throng: with this view I accepted of an invitation to dine with one, whose open easy manner left me no room to doubt of a cordial welcome. Sir Thomas Friendly, an intimate friend of my late uncle's, with two sons and five daughters, all grown up, and living with their mother and a maiden sister of Sir Thomas's. Conscious of my unpolished gait, I for some time took private lessons of a professor, who teaches "grown gentlemen to dance." Having by this means acquired the art of walking without tottering, and learning to make a bow, I boldly ventured to obey the baronet's invitation to a family dinner, not doubting but my new acquirements would enable me to see the ladies with tolerable intrepidity but, alas! how vain are all the hopes of theory, when unsupported by habitual practice. As I approached the house, a dinner-bell alarmed my fears, lest I had spoiled the dinner by want of punctuality; impressed with this idea, I blushed the deepest crimson, as my name was repeatedly announced by the several livery-servants, who ushered me into the library, hardly knowing what or whom I saw. At my first entrance, I summoned all my fortitude, and made my new-learnt bow to Lady Friendly; but, unfortunately, in bringing my left foot to the third position, I trod upon the gouty toe of poor Sir Thomas, who had followed close to my heels, to be the nomenclator of the family. The confusion this occasioned in me is hardly to be conceived, since none but bashful men can judge of my distress; and of that description, the number, I believe, is very small. The baronet's politeness, by degrees, dissipated my concern, and I was astonished to see how far good breeding could enable him to support his feelings, and to appear with perfect ease, after so painful an accident.

The cheerfulness of her ladyship, and the familiar chat of the young ladies, insensibly led me to throw off my reserve and sheepishness, till, at length, I ventured to join in conversation, and even to start fresh subjects. The library being richly furnished with books in elegant bindings, and observing an edition of Xenophon, in sixteen volumes, which (as I had never before heard of) greatly excited my curiosity. I rose up to examine what it could be; Sir Thomas saw what I was about, and, as I suppose, willing to save me the trouble, rose to take down the book, which made me more eager to prevent him; and hastily laying my hand on the first volume, I pulled it forcibly; but, lo! instead of books, a board, which by leather and gilding had been made to look like sixteen volumes, came tumbling down, and unluckily pitched upon a Wedgewood inkstand on the table, under it. In vain did Sir Thomas assure me, there was no harm; I saw the ink streaming from an inlaid table on the Turkey carpet, and, scarce knowing what I did, I attempted to stop its progress with my cambric handkerchief. In the height of this confusion, we were informed that dinner was served up, and I with joy perceived that the bell, which at first had so alarmed my fears, was only the half-hour dinner-bell.

In walking through the hall and suite of apartments to the dining-room, I had time to collect my scattered senses, and was desired to take my seat between Lady Friendly and her eldest daughter, at the table. Since the fall of the wooden Xenophon, my face had been continually burning, like a firebrand; and I was just beginning to recover myself, and to feel comfortably cool, when an unlooked-for accident rekindled all my heat and blushes. Having set my plate of soup too near the edge of the table, in bowing to Miss Dinah, who politely complimented the pattern of my waistcoat, I tumbled the whole scalding contents into my lap. In spite of an immediate supply of napkins to wipe the surface of my clothes, my black silk breeches were not stout enough to save me from the painful effects of this sudden fomentation, and for some minutes my legs and thighs seemed stewing in a boiling caldron; but recollecting how Sir Thomas had disguised his torture, when I trod upon his toe, I firmly bore my pain in silence, and sat with my lower extremities parboiled, amidst the stifled giggling of the ladies and servants.

I will not relate the several blunders which I made during the first course, or the distress occasioned by my being desired to carve a fowl, or help to various dishes that stood near me, spilling a sauce-boat, and knocking down a salt-cellar; rather let me hasten to the second course, "where fresh disasters overwhelmed me quite."

I had a piece of rich sweet pudding on my fork, when Miss Louisa Friendly begged to trouble me for a pigeon that stood near me. In my haste, scarcely knowing what I did, I whipped the pudding into my mouth, hot as a burning coal; it was impossible to conceal my agony—my eyes were starting from their sockets. At last, in spite of shame and resolution, I was obliged to drop the cause of my torment on my plate. Sir Thomas and the ladies all compassionated my misfortune, and each advised a different application; one recommended oil, another water, but all agreed that wine was the best for drawing out fire, and a glass of sherry was brought me from the side-board, which I snatched up with eagerness: but, oh! how shall I tell the sequel? whether the butler by accident mistook, or purposely designed to drive me mad, he gave me the strongest brandy, with which I filled my mouth, already flayed and blistered. Totally unused to ardent spirits, with my tongue, throat, and palate as raw as beef, what could I do? I could not swallow;

THE BASHFUL MAN'S STORY. 35

but clapping my hands upon my mouth, the cursed liquor squirted through my nose and fingers like a fountain, over all the dishes; and I, crushed by bursts of laughter from all quarters. In vain did Sir Thomas reprimand the servants, and Lady Friendly chide her daughters; for the measure of my shame and their diversion was not yet complete. To relieve me from the intolerable state of perspiration which this accident had caused, without considering what I did, I wiped my face with that ill-fated handkerchief, which was still wet from the consequences of the fall of Xenophon, and covered all my features with streaks of ink in every direction. The baronet himself could not support this shock, but joined his lady in the general laugh; while I sprung from the table in despair, rushed out of the house, and ran home in an agony of confusion and disgrace, which the most poignant sense of guilt could have excited.

Thus, without having deviated from the path of moral rectitude, I am suffering torments like a "goblin damned." The lower half of me has been almost boiled, my tongue and mouth grilled, and I bear the mark of Cain upon my forehead; yet these are but trifling considerations, to the everlasting shame which I must feel, whenever this adventure shall be mentioned. Perhaps, by your assistance, when my neighbors know how much I feel on the occasion, they will spare a bashful man, and, as I am just informed my poultice is ready, I trust you will excuse the haste in which I retire.

THE MATTER-OF-FACT MAN.

Anon.

I am what the old women call an "Odd Fish." I do nothing under heaven without a motive—never. I attempt nothing, unless I think there is a probability of my succeeding. I ask no favors when I think they are not deserved; and finally, I don't wait upon the girls when I think my attentions would be disagreeable. I am a matter-of-fact man, I am. I do every thing seriously. I once offered to attend a young lady home; I did it seriously; that is, I meant to wait on her home if she wanted me. She accepted my offer; I went home with her, and it has ever since been an enigma with me whether she wanted me or not. I bade her good night, and she said not a word. I met her next morning, and I said not a word. I met her again, and she gave me two hours' talk. It struck me as curious. She feared I was offended, she said, and could not, for the life of her, conceive why. She begged me to explain, but would not give me a chance to do so. She said she hoped I wouldn't be offended, asked me to call, and it has ever since been a mystery to me whether she wanted me or not.

Once I saw a lady at her window. I thought I would call. I did. I inquired for the lady, and was told she was not at home. I expected she was, I went away thinking so. I rather think so still. I met her again—she was offended—said I had not been neighborly. She reproached me for my negligence; said she thought I had been unkind. And I've ever since wondered whether she thought so or not.

A lady once said to me that she should like to be married if she could get a good, congenial husband who would make her happy, or at least try to. She was not difficult to please, she said. I said I should like to get married, too, if I could find a wife that would try to make me happy. She said Umph, and looked as if she meant what she said. She did. For when I asked her if she thought she could not be persuaded to marry me, she said she would rather be excused. I have often wondered why I excused her.

A good many things of this kind have happened to me, that are doubtful, wonderful, mysterious. What is it, then, that causes doubt and mystery to attend the ways of men? It is the want of fact. This is a matter-of-fact world, and in order to act well in it, we must deal in a matter-of-fact way.

RICH AND POOR.

Joseph Barber.

"Men are born equal;" Jefferson, the Sage,
Upon our history's initial page,
Inscribed that dictum;
But we who live in later times amend
The "declaration" of our patriot friend
With a *postscriptum*.

We deem, like him, swart Labor's son and heir,
And wealth's soft bantling, of *one earthenware*,
But mark the sequel:
One's meanly clothed in threadbare suit forlorn,
The other flaunts in velvet, lace, and lawn;
Are they then equal?

Five thousand children in New York, each year,
Gasp for bare life, in cellars damp and drear,
'Neath the street level.
Deprived of sunshine, chill'd with vapor-blights,
Say what are *their* "inalienable rights,"
Social and civil?

The right to starve, the right to beg, to float
Among the city's scum — perchance to vote
Some day as "freemen."
Ah! yes, the *polls* their sovereignty declare,
Not so — in sordid chains they're oft led there
By Faction's Demon.

"The rich and poor are equal," says the State,
But the strong laws of destiny and fate,
O'erride its polity.
Both have a right to *seek* for "happiness;"
But, with such different chances of success,
Where's the *equality*?

Here wealth like a Colossus doth bestride
With legs of gold, the sorrow-troubled tide
Of Want and Squalor.
Nay, more, Law, Justice, oft becomes the tool

Of that bright tyrant, callous, calm, and cool,
Almighty Dollar!

"All men are equal," where? Why, in their dust,
Your worm cares little for your "upper crust!"
(What impropriety!)
And heaven receives alike all spirits pure,
On equal terms, and heaven is therefore sure
Of good society.

SEEING THE ECLIPSE.

Anon.

[To be spoken without gesture, as if the speaker were telling a friend his experience.]

Did you ever see an eclipse? No? Well, you *did* miss a sight, got up for the especial benefit of darkies, perhaps, but every white man, of good *standing*, could enjoy it—*if* he was up. I'll tell you *my* experience, and you may judge what you have lost by not seeing the eclipse.

Well, I got up at three o'clock Wednesday morning. Looked for the sun, but couldn't find it. Concluded that I was up too early. Went to bed.

Got up again at half-past five. Saw something they called the sun. Looked red. Went down town. Sun looked whiter and bright as a tin pan. Thought I would go home and get breakfast. Noticed the breakfast-room looked dark. Opened the blinds when it looked lighter.

Seven o'clock. Went down town again. Sun shining very bright. Tried to look at it but couldn't. Thought I would take a glass. Took one. Smoked it. Thought that I could see better, but wasn't satisfied. Didn't see any eclipse.

Eight o'clock. Took another glass, thinking it might be a better one. Smoked. Could see a patch on the sun's face. Grew bigger. Took another glass—smoked. Looked first-rate.

Half-past eight. Things didn't look right, but could see something. Thought the trouble might be in the last glass. Took another. Saw the biggest kind of an eclipse. Saw the sun and moon. Took another glass and looked again. Saw two suns. Smoked and took another glass. Saw two suns and two moons. Took another glass. Five or six suns and ten or fifteen moons all mixed up and seemed to be drunk.

Nine o'clock. Couldn't see much of any thing. Concluded I must be sun-struck. Thought I would go home. Saw an omnibus, and thought I would get in. Turned out to be one of Swartz's what-d'ye-call-it. Tried another, and got in. Went home in a coal cart. Think eclipses are humbugs, besides making people have headaches.

THE BEAUTIES OF THE LAW.

[Recited in the character of Counsellor Quirk.]

Farmer A. and Farmer B. were good neighbors. Farmer A. was seized or possessed of a white bull; Farmer B. was seized or possessed of, or otherwise well entitled to, a ferry-boat. Farmer B. having made his boat fast to a post on shore, by means of a piece of hay, twisted rope-fashion, or, as we say, *vulgato vocto*, a hay-band, went up to town to get his dinner, which was also very natural for a hungry man to do. In the mean time Farmer A.'s white bull came down to the town to look for his dinner, which was also very natural for a hungry bull to do; the said white bull, discovering, seeing, and spying out, some turnips in the bottom of the ferry-boat, the bull scrambled into the ferry-boat aforesaid, eat up the turnips, and, to make an end of his meal, fell to work upon the hay-band. The ferry-boat being ate from its moorings, floated down the river with the white bull in it: it struck against a rock, which beat a hole in the bottom of the boat, and tossed the bull overboard; whereupon, the owner of the bull brought his action against the boat, for running away with the bull. The owner of the boat brought his action against the bull, for running away with the boat; and thus notice of the trial was given, Bullum *versus* Boatum—Boatum *versus* Bullum. Now the counsel for the bull began with saying: "Your Honor, and you, Gentlemen of the Jury, we are counsel in this cause for the bull. We are indicted for running away with the boat. Now, your Honor, your Honor may have heard of running horses, but never of running bulls before. Now, your Honor, I humbly submit to your Honor, the bull could no more have run away with the boat, than a man in a coach may be said to run away with the horses; therefore, your Honor, how can an action be maintained against that which is not actionable? How can we punish what is not punishable? How can we eat what is not eatable? Or, how can we drink what is not drinkable? Or, as the law says, how can we think on what is not thinkable? Therefore, your Honor, as we are counsel in this cause for the bull, if the jury should bring the bull in guilty, the jury will be guilty of a bull." The learned counsel for the boat, in the cross-action of Bullum *versus* Boatum, observed, that the bull should be nonsuited, because, in his declaration, he had omitted to state or specify what color he was; for thus wisely and thus learnedly spoke the counsel: "My Lord, if the bull was of no color he must be of some color; and if he was not of any color, what color could the bull be?" I overruled this motion myself, by observing the bull was a white bull, and that white is no color: besides, as I told my brethren, they should not trouble their heads to talk of color in the law, for the law can color any thing. The cause being afterwards left to a reference, upon the award, both bull and boat were acquitted, it being proved that the tide of the river carried them both away; upon which I

THE BEAUTIES OF THE LAW. 41

gave it, as my opinion, that as the tide of the river carried both bull and boat away, both bull and boat had a good action against the water-bailiff. My opinion being taken, an action was issued, and, upon the traverse, this point of law arose: how, wherefore, and whether, why, when, and whatsoever, whereas, and whereby, as the boat was not a *compos mentis* evidence, how could an oath be administered? That point was soon settled by Boatum's attorney declaring, that for his client he would swear any thing. The water-bailiff's charter was then read, taken out of the original law Latin, which set forth in their declaration, that they were carried away either by the tide of flood, or the tide of ebb, the charter of the water-bailiff was as follows: Aquæ bailiffi est magistratus in choisi, sapor omnibus, fishibus, qui haberunt finnos et scalos, claws, shells, et talos, qui surmare in freshibus, vel saltibus riveris, lakos, pondis, canalibus et well boats, sive oysteri, shrimpini, catinos, sturgeoni, shadini, herringi, crabi, snaperini, flatini, sharkus; that is, not flat-fish alone, but flats and sharps both together. But now comes the nicety of the law, the law is as nice as a new-laid egg, and not to be understood by addle-headed people. Bullum and Boatum mentioned both ebb and flood to avoid quibbling, but it being proved that they were carried away, neither by the flood, nor by the tide of ebb, but exactly upon the top of high water, they were consequently nonsuited; but such was the lenity and perfection of our laws, that upon their paying all the costs, they were allowed to begin again, *de novo*.

GE-LANG! GIT UP!
New Orleans Delta.

The drops of rain were falling fast,
When up through Camp-street quickly pass'd,
An omnibus, whose driver sung,
In accents of the Celtic tongue—
Ge-lang! git up!

His mules were lank, his whip was long;
He touch'd them with a biting thong,
And as they switch'd their threadbare tails,
This sound the listening ear assails—
Ge-lang! git up!

Along the street, on every side,
Were damp ones waiting for a ride;
They call'd, they yell'd, they raised a fuss,
But cried the driver of the 'bus.
Ge-lang! git up!

"Hold on! hold on!" an old man said,
And waved his hand above his head;
Crack went the whip, and all could hear
A sharp sound echoing on the ear—
Ge-lang! git up!

"Stop, driver, stop!" a maiden call'd
"Stop, stop!" a dozen voices bawl'd
The driver look'd on neither side,
But still in clarion voice replied—
Ge-lang! git up!

Far up the street a sound was heard,
And through the distance came a word
That fell on many a waiting soul
Like Hope's lugubrious funeral toll—
Ge-lang! git up!

That night the driver went to bed;
All through his troubled sleep he said
The same strange words which he had flung

GE-LANG! GIT UP!

All day from his Jehuic tongue—
Ge-lang! git up!

THE RATS OF LIFE.
Charles T. Congdon.

Rats! rats! rats!
Pen-and-ink rats in their holes on high,
Writing libels for fools to buy;
Squabbling ever—the same old tune—
The hinted lie, or the broad lampoon!
Rats whose virtue can never fail,
Though each one carries his price on his tail;
Some bite like scorpions—some like gnats;
Know ye the names of the Editor Rats?

Rats! rats! rats!
Rats that the belfried churches nurse,
Drearily drawling chapter and verse;
Offering ever for human ills
Only the barren letter that kills;
Gnawing the Ark of the Covenant through,
From velvet cushion to padded pew;
Beating the dust to blind the flats!
Know ye the names of the Reverend Rats?

Rats! rats! rats!
Rats in ermine holding moot,
With law in parcels at prices to suit;
Shaping, inventing to cover the case,
Precedent musty or dictum base,
Gad! how they gibber to suitors below:
"If so be it thus, why then thus be it so!"
Leges non curant—verhum sat!
Know ye the name of the Legal Rat?

Rats! rats! rats!
Rats in the ancient Temple of Mind—
Mumbling maggots and munching rind!
Scrubbing and patching, splicing and jointing,
With particles Greek and with Hebrew pointing.
Proving virtue itself a sin,
By a comma left out or a colon left in;
Of guesses and glosses the autocrats:

THE RATS OF LIFE.

Know ye the names of the Learned Rats?

Rats! rats! rats!
By beds where the dying pant for life!
How snug they stand with lancet and knife;
While the vampyre tugs at the fluttering heart,
How they jabber jargon of middle-aged art!
Soothing pain when 'tis savage and strong
By naming it something Latin and long!
A grain of this and a scruple of that! —
Know ye the name of the Medical Rat?

Rats! rats! rats!
Rats that run in the month of May
Rats of reform and right are they!
Rats who believe the hottest of speeches
Soonest the shame and sorrow reaches;
Generous rats whose chiefest delight
Is to set the order of Providence right;
Lean, or hairy, or greasy, or fat,
Know ye the name of the Platform Rat?

Rats! rats! rats!
Oh, Truth and Justice, and Common-Sense
When will you drive this rat-tribe hence?
Bait 'em and beat 'em! hurry 'em! skurry 'em!
With satire and scorn and laughter flurry 'em!
In hole and corner and cranny to hide,
The Flunkey Rat, and the Rat of Pride,
Selfishness, Pedantry, Cant, and all that,
Till nobody hears of a single Rat!

"THE CREOWNIN' GLORY OF THE UNITED STATES."

Knickerbocker Magazine.

My Hearers:—My text ain't in Worcester's Pictorial, nor Webster's big quarto; but it is in the columns of the Bunkum Flagstaff and Independent Echo—"*Edication is the Creownin' Glory of the United'n States'n.*" Thar ain't a feller in all this great and glorious Republic but has studed readin', ritin', and 'rithmetic. Thar ain't a youngster so big that you couldn't drown him in a spit-box but what has read Shakspeare's gogerphy, and knows that all the world is a stage, with two poles instead of one like a common stage; and that it keeps goin' reound and reound on its own axis, not axin' nothin' o' nobody; for "*Edication is the Creownin' Glory of the United'n States'n.*" Who was it that, durin' the great and glorious Revolution, by his eloquence quenched the spirit of Toryism? An American citizen. Who was it that knocked thunder out of the clouds, and took a streak o' greased lightnin' for a tail to his kite? An American citizen. Who was it that invented the powder that will kill a cockroach, if you put a little on its tail and then tread on it? Who was it that discovered the Fat Boy, and captured the wild and ferocious *What Is It?* An American citizen! Oh, it's a smashin' big thing to be an American citizen! King David would have been an American citizen, and the Queen of Sheba would have been naturalized, if it could a bin did; for "*Edication is the Creownin' Glory of the United'n States'n.*" When you and I shall be no more; when this glorious Union shall have gone to etarnal smash; when Barnum shall have secured his last curiosity at a great expense; then will the historian dip his pen in a georgious bottle of blue-black ink, and write—"*Edication was the Creownin' Glory of the United'n States'n.*"

THREE FOOLS.
C. H. Spurgeon.

I will show you three fools. One is yonder soldier, who has been wounded on the field of battle—grievously wounded, well-nigh unto death. The soldier asks him a question. Listen, and judge of his folly! What question does he ask? Does he raise his eyes with eager anxiety and inquire if the wound be mortal, if the practitioner's skill can suggest the means of healing, or if the remedies are within reach and the medicine at hand? No, nothing of the sort. Strange to tell, he asks: "Can you inform me with what sword I was wounded, and by what Russian I have been thus grievously mauled? I want," he adds, "to learn every minute particular respecting the origin of my wound." The man is delirious, his head is affected! Surely such questions at such a time are proof enough that he is bereft of his senses.

There is another fool. The storm is raging, the ship is flying impetuously before the gale, the dark scud moves swiftly overhead, masts are creaking, the sails are rent to rags, and still the gathering tempest grows more fierce. Where is the captain? Is he busily engaged on the deck, is he manfully facing the danger, and skillfully suggesting means to avert it? No, sir, he has retired to his cabin; and there, with studious thoughts and crazy fancies, he is speculating on the place where this storm took its rise. "It is mysterious, this wind; no one ever yet," he says, "has been able to discover it." And so, reckless of the vessel, the lives of the passengers, and his own life, he is careful only to solve his curious question. The man is mad, sir; take the rudder from his hand; he is clean gone mad!

The third fool I shall doubtless find among yourselves. You are sick and wounded with sin, you are in a storm and hurricane of Almighty vengeance, and yet the question which you would ask of me this morning would be: "Sir, what is the origin of evil?" You are mad, sir, spiritually mad; that is not the question you would ask if you were in a sane and healthy state of mind. Your question would be: "How can I get rid of the evil?" Not, "How did it come into the world?" but, "How am I to escape from it?" Not, "How is it that fire descended from heaven upon Sodom?" but, "How may I, like Lot, escape out of the city to a Zoar?" Not, "How is it that I am sick?" but, "Are there medicines that will heal me? Is there a physician to be found that can restore my soul to health?" Ah! you trifle with subtleties, while you neglect certainties.

WASHINGTON.

Hon. Thomas S. Bocock, Feb. 22d, 1860.

As certain vegetable products are the natural growth of particular soils, at particular times, so some men spring almost necessarily out of certain forms of civilization, and stand as the representatives of the times and countries in which they live.

Pericles, able, accomplished, magnificent, was the representative man of Athens in the time of her highest civilization and prosperity. Richard I. was the representative man of England in the days of chivalry, and Charles II. in the days of gallantry. These men could scarcely have lived in any other age or clime. So Washington could scarcely have had his existence in any other time or country. He could no more have been an Italian of the middle ages, than Machiavelli could have been an American, or Cæsar Borgia an Englishman: no more than the Parthenon could have been a Gothic cathedral, or Westminster Abbey a Grecian temple. He was at once the offspring and the type of American civilization at his time. He was our great forest-bred cavalier, with all the high honor of his ancestral stock of De Wessingtons, with all the hardy firmness of a pioneer, and with all the kindly courtesy of his native State. Among the Adamses and Hancocks, the Lees and Henrys, the Sumpters and Rutledges of that day, he stood forth prominently as the representative man, and as the exemplar of our Revolution, just as that triplex monstrosity of Danton, Marat, and Robespierre, was the exemplar of the French.

He was a man of firm adherence to principle. We fought for principle in the revolutionary struggle. He was a man of signal moderation. Such was the spirit of our contest. He had great self-control. Unlike other revolutions, ours advanced not one step beyond the point proposed. Having reached that, it subsided as easily, as gracefully, and as quietly as though the voice of Omnipotence itself had spoken to the great deep of our society, saying: *"Peace, be still."*

Could he have lived in ancient days, the strains of immortal verse would have told his deeds, and fond adherents would have numbered him among the gods.

Those days are past; but we have yet hearts to admire, and pens to record, and tongues to praise his private virtues and his public worth. And when century after century shall have rolled by, bearing its fruits into the bosom of the past; even when men shall look back to this time, through the haze and mist of a remote and far-off antiquity, if this shall still be a land of freemen, this day shall still be fondly cherished as the anniversary of the birth of Washington; increased reverence shall attend his character, and thickening honors shall cluster around his name.

Upon this representative and similitude of the great and honored dead, which we this day put forth before the world, the winds shall blow, the rains shall fall, and the storms shall beat, but it shall stand unhurt amid them all. So shall it be with the fame of him whose image it is. The breath of unfriendly criticism may blow upon it; the storms that betoken moral or social change may break upon it; but it shall stand firmly fixed in the hearts and memories of every true and honest and liberty-loving man who inhabits our land or cherishes our institutions.

The inhabitants of this city, as they behold this statue, day after day, will look upon it as the Palladium of their privileges, and the silent guardian of their prosperity. And the thousands and tens of thousands, that from every nation, kingdom, and tongue, yearly go forth to gaze upon and admire the wonders of the earth, when they shall come up to this "Mecca of the mind," shall pause with reverential awe, as they gaze upon this similitude of the mighty Washington.

Year after year shall that dumb image tell its eloquent story of patriotism, devotion, and self-sacrifice; year after year shall it teach its holy lesson of duty and of faith; with generation after generation shall it plead for institutions founded in wisdom, and a country bought with blood. To the clouds and storms that gather over and break upon it, it will tell of the clouds and storms through which its great antitype did pass, in his devoted course on earth; and when the great luminary of the heavens, descending with his golden shower of beams like imperial Jove, shall wrap it in its warm embrace, it shall tell the sun that He who gave him his beams and bade him shine, has decreed that one day the darkness of eternal night shall settle on his face; but then the spirit of the mighty Washington, basking in an eternal sunlight above, shall still

> "A darkening universe defy,
> To quench his immortality,
> Or shake his trust in God."

THE SAME.
Ibid

Think, then, of the eminent statesmen whose talents have illustrated and qualities ennobled their age and country. I will not attempt to name them; but who is there among them all who, having the wisdom always to perceive, Lad, at the same time, the sense of duty to carry out, the best interests of the country? Consider, if you please, how Richelieu lived, and how Wolsey died; and tell me, then, if these were such as Washington. I will not equal him with the Scripture patriarchs. It would be wrong so to do. What of mere mortality could equal the firmness of Moses, as he came down from Sinai, his face all glowing from the presence of his God? What could equal the faith of Abraham, as he tracked his lonely pilgrimage through the plains of Shinar, seeking a land that he knew not of? These pictures have a far-off, haze-enveloped, oriental background. They are drawn with the pencil of inspiration, and colored with the hues of heaven. I could not say that they correctly represent Washington in any phase of his character. But I will say that, in duty and in faith, he approached them more nearly than any other hero-statesman of whom I have any knowledge. I would not deal in any exaggeration, but I desire to be just.

Washington may have had ambition, but it was not of that stamp that made the angels fall. He loved popularity, but not to gratify a vulgar vanity. His ambition was for his country's good. He took office to achieve a great end. When that was accomplished, he withdrew gladly to that retirement which was ever grateful to his heart, and which, in all circumstances and conditions in which he might be placed, always stretched out before him, in the future, as the calm and peaceful haven of his hopes. Had he been less a good man, he would not thus have desired retirement, for none but a good man could so love the calm delights of privacy and the pure joys of the domestic circle and the family fireside. Had he been not so much a great one, he would never have left his home.

Strange decree of fate! that in this Western world, but recently known to civilization, and only partially reclaimed from the savages; over which the dull oblivion of unnumbered centuries had not yet ceased to brood; without literature, without polite arts, without settled social organization, without position among nations—that in such a land, almost unknown and utterly uncared for, there should have arisen a man who was destined to equal, in the estimation of the virtuous and the good, all ancient glory and all modern fame.

The verdict of the French philosopher, Guizot, pronounced in view of his whole record, was, that "of all great men he was the most virtuous and the most

THE SAME.

fortunate—in this world God has no higher favors to bestow;" while the great English orator, jurist, and statesman, Lord Brougham, has declared that "until time shall be no more, will a test of the progress which our race has made in wisdom and virtue be derived from the veneration paid to the immortal name of Washington."

THE SAME.
Ibid.

Had Washington never lived, what would have been the result of our revolutionary struggle? Had he died immediately after the close of the war, what would have been the fate of our governmental experiment? These are speculations which it will never be allowed us, in this life, to solve. As, in the one case, we can not say that the struggle would not ultimately have ended triumphantly, so, in the other, we do not know that our present form of government would not have been successfully established. For myself, I doubt the latter proposition fully as much as the former. Under another man, as first President, the fury of party strife would have been far greater, and sectional discord much stronger. Insurrectionary movements would have been more numerous and difficult of suppression, and foreign jealousy more bold and effective.

Though the ship of state may have ultimately made the port, it is certain that she would have encountered more adverse currents, and been tossed upon more tempestuous seas. The political tempest which was passing over the country at the time of his death, gives some faint idea of what might have been expected, without him, in the earlier and more unsettled state of our institutions. The immortal legacy which, in his "*Farewell Address,*" he gave to the country on his final retirement, has already exhausted eulogy. The patriot heart has often kindled over it in the past, and will do so forever in the future. It will go down to the remotest posterity which shall inhabit this land of liberty, as an inestimable compend of whatever is true in wisdom, holy in patriotism, and far-seeing in statesmanship. Would that its doctrines were not only infused into every mind, but engraved upon every heart! Would that its lesson of "*equal laws*" involving equal burdens and equal benefits, equal duties and equal protection, and of strict regard for constitutional limitation in all cases, was made the basis of all our political action! Then, indeed, would party feuds and sectional animosities be allayed. A spirit of mutual respect and fraternal concord would fill the land with the fruits of peace, prosperity, and happiness. With all our fertile soil, salubrious climate, skillful industry, and enriching trade, this only is needed to usher in, amid shouts of triumph and songs of rejoicing, the political millennium of our land.

Now, though withdrawn from public position, his controlling sense of duty made Washington still anxious for his country, and ready to render any service which might appear incumbent on him. So, when it seemed that a war with France was inevitable, old man as he was, enshrined as he was in the hearts of his countrymen, with nothing more of fame to attain, and nothing more of glory to covet, from a pure sense of duty, he agreed to take charge of the armies of the nation, and to imperil life, reputation, every thing, for his country's good. The occasion for his services did not arise; but the certainty that it would not was scarcely manifest, when death came to summon him to the "mansions of eternal rest."

It is allowed to few men to carry on a revolution, and to see it successfully terminated in the independence of a nation. Fewer still, perhaps, are permitted to inaugurate a new government, and witness its firm establishment in the freedom of the people. Washington had the singular good fortune to do both, and to die at last at home and in the bosom of his family.

Hero! Patriot! Sage! If there be one title more pure, more lofty, more noble than all others, by that title I would name him. To whom shall we liken him, or with whom shall he be compared? There is the long list of military heroes, in ancient and modern times. Let them pass in solemn procession across the stage, each bearing the light of his past life, like the solemn procession of torch-bearers in the sacred mysteries of Eleusis. Gaze on them as they pass! Great, illustrious, resplendent! There are Alexander and Hannibal, Scylla and Cæsar, Charlemagne and Marlborough, Bonaparte and Wellington. Which one of them all that has not a record marked by some weakness, or marred by some crime? Love of glory, lust of dominion, or greed of gain, is written by the pen of history upon the escutcheon of all.

OUR GREAT INHERITANCE.
John J. Crittenden, 1860.

We have the greatest country on the face of the earth. Let not our minds be so distracted by mere party strife and confusion that we shall see our government fall to pieces before our eyes, and sacrifice our country to our party instead of being ready at all times to sacrifice our party to our country. After we become the slave of party, we dare not, in the presence of any danger to the country, turn our backs to our parties, and say that we have a country that demands our services, and to it will we give them. Are we now unable to do this? Have we lost this spirit? has it gone from among us?

Providence has given this great country to us. Our wise and valiant forefathers gave us liberty and established a government for us. Let us take care of it—take care of the Constitution and the Union. That is all we require. We have before us the prospect of a glory unknown to other nations—a prospect in which our land will become the glory of the earth. Neither Rome nor any of the great empires of antiquity or of modern times can compare with what we shall be at no distant day. We are now thirty millions strong, yet we have been but eighty years in existence as a free nation. From the year 1776 down to the present time, God Almighty has blessed us above all other people and all other nations. Where shall we be thirty years hence, if such prosperity attend us? A great nation of one hundred million souls, with not enough then to develop all our resources. Every man free to think, free to speak, free to act, free to work. What must this mighty freedom produce with this mighty concurrence of hearts, of heads, of hands! What navies, what armies, what cities! Let us lift ourselves to the contemplation of what our children will be. Shall we not leave them a legacy as great as that our fathers left us? Let the contemplation of the mighty destinies involved in our Confederacy engage us until we absorb the genius of this Republic and its Constitution. Let it enter into all our motives of public action, that we may no longer be the tools and slaves of parties, of party platforms, and of party conventions.

EULOGIUM ON HENRY CLAY.
Lincoln, 1852.

On the 4th day of July, 1776, the people of a few feeble and oppressed colonies of Great Britain, inhabiting a portion of the Atlantic coast of North America, publicly declared their National Independence, and made their appeal to the justice of their cause, and to the God of battles, for the maintenance of that declaration. That people were few in numbers, and without resources, save only their wise heads and stout hearts. Within the first year of that declared independence, and while its maintenance was yet problematic—while the bloody struggle between those resolute rebels and their haughty would-be masters, was still waging, of undistinguished parents, and in an obscure district of one of those colonies, Henry Clay was born. The infant nation and the infant child began the race together. For three-quarters of a century they have traveled hand in hand. They have been companions ever. The nation has passed its peril, and is free, prosperous, and powerful. The child has reached his manhood, his middle age, his old age, and is dead. In all that has concerned the nation the man ever sympathized, and now the nation mourns for the man.

But do we realize that Henry Clay is dead? Who can realize that never again that majestic form shall rise in the council-chamber of his country, to beat back the storms of anarchy which may threaten, or pour the oil of peace upon the troubled billows, as they rage and menace around? Who can realize that the workings of that mighty mind have ceased—that the throbbings of that gallant heart are stilled—that the mighty sweep of that graceful arm will be felt no more, and the magic of that eloquent tongue, which spake as spake no other tongue besides, is hushed—hushed forever? Who can realize that freedom's champion—the champion of a civilized world, and of all tongues and kindred and people, has indeed fallen? Alas! in those dark hours of peril and dread which our land has experienced, and which she may be called to experience again—to whom now may her people look up for that counsel and advice, which only wisdom and experience and patriotism can give, and which only the undoubting confidence of a nation will receive?

But Henry Clay is dead. His long and eventful life is closed. Our country is prosperous and powerful; but could it have been quite all it has been, and is, and is to be, without Henry Clay? Such a man the times have demanded, and such, in the Providence of God, was given us. But although his form is lifeless, his name will live and be loved and venerated in both hemispheres. For it is

"One of the few, the immortal names,

That were not born to die."

OHIO.

Bancroft's Oration at Cleveland, Sept. 10th, 1860.

Ohio rises before the world as the majestic witness to beneficent reality of the democratic principle. A commonwealth younger in years than he who addresses you, not long ago having no visible existence but in the emigrant wagons, now numbers almost as large a population as that of all England when it gave birth to Raleigh, and Bacon, and Shakspeare, and began, its continuous attempts at colonizing America. Each one of her inhabitants gladdens in the fruit of his own toil. She possesses wealth that must be computed by thousands of millions; and her frugal, industrious, and benevolent people, at once daring and prudent, unfettered in the use of their faculties, restless in enterprise, do not squander the accumulations of their industry in vain show, but ever go on to render the earth more productive, more beautiful, and more convenient to man; mastering for mechanical purposes the unwasting forces of nature; keeping exemplary good faith with their public creditors; building in half a century more churches than all England has raised since this continent was discovered; endowing and sustaining universities and other seminaries of learning. Conscious of the dynamic power of mind in action as the best of fortresses, Ohio keeps no standing army but that of her school-teachers, of whom she pays more than 20,000; she provides a library for every school-district; she counts among her citizens more than 300,000 men who can bear arms, and she has more than twice that number of children registered as students in her public schools. Here the purity of domestic morals is maintained by the virtue and dignity of woman.

In the heart of the temperate zone of this continent, in the land of the corn, of wheat, and the vine, the eldest daughter of the Ordinance of 1787, already the young mother of other commonwealths, that bid fair to vie with her in beauty, rises in her loveliness and glory, crowned with cities, and challenges the admiration of the world. Hither should come the political skeptic, who, in his despair, is ready to strand the ship of state; for here he may learn how to guide it safely on the waters. Should some modern Telemachus, heir to an island empire, touch these shores, here he may observe the vitality and strength of the principle of popular power; take from the book of experience the lesson that in public affairs great and happy results follow in proportion to faith in the efficacy of that principle, and learn to rebuke ill-advised counselors who pronounce the most momentous and most certain of political truths a delusion and a failure.

OLIVER HAZARD PERRY.
Ibid.

This anniversary of the great action of Oliver Hazard Perry is set apart for inaugurating a monument to his fame. Who has not heard how gallantly, forty-seven years ago, the young hero, still weak from a wasting fever, led his squadron to battle? As if shielded by a higher power, he encountered death on his right hand, and death on his left, ever in advance, almost alone for two hours fighting his ship, till it became a wreck, so that but one of its guns could be used any longer, and more than four-fifths of his crew lay around him wounded or killed; then unharmed, standing as beseemed his spirit, he passed in a boat to the uninjured Niagara, unfurled his flag, bore down within pistol-shot of his enemy, poured into them broadsides starboard and broadsides port, and while the sun was still high above the horizon, left no office to be done but that of mercy to the vanquished. If the comparison does not seem fanciful, I will call his conduct during those eventful hours a complete lyric poem, perfect in all its parts. Though he was carried away and raised above himself by the power with which he was possessed, the passion of his inspiration was tempered by the serene self-possession of his faultless courage; his will had the winged rapidity of fiery thought, and yet observed with deliberateness the combinations of harmony and the proportions of measured order.

Nor may you omit due honors to the virtues of the unrecorded dead; not as mourners who require consolation, but with a clear perception of the glory of their end. The debt of nature all must pay. To die, if need be, in defense of the country is a common obligation; it is granted to few to exchange life for a victory so full of benefits to their fellow-men. These are the disinterested, unnamed martyrs, who, without hope, or fame, or gain, gave up their lives in testimony to the all pleading love of country, and left to our statesmen the lesson to demand of others nothing but what is right, and to submit to no wrong.

"We have met the enemy," were Perry's words as he reported the result of the battle. And who was that enemy? A nation speaking another tongue? A state abandoned to the caprices of despotism? A people inimical to human freedom? No! they were the nation from whom most of us sprung, using the same copious language, cherishing after their fashion the love of liberty, enjoying internally the freest government that the world had known before our own. But the external policy of their government has been less controlled by regard for right than their domestic administration; and a series of wanton aggression, upon us, useless to England, condemned by her own statesmen and judges as violations of the law of nature and the law of nations, forced into a conflict two peoples whose common sympathies should never have been disturbed. And is this aggressive system forever to be adventured by her rulers? How long is the overshadowing aristocratic element in her government to stand between the natural affections of kindred nations.

OUR DOMAIN.
Ibid.

Even now a British minister, whose past career gave hope of a greater fairness, is renewing the old system of experiments on the possible contingency of the pusillanimity, the indifference, or the ignorance of some future American administration, and disputes our boundary in the Northwest, though the words of the treaty are too plain to be perverted, and though the United States claims no more than the British secretary of state, who offered the treaty, explained as its meaning before it was signed. British soldiers are now encamped on part of our territory which bears the name of Washington. With a moderation that should have commanded respect, the United States waived their better claim to Vancouver, and even to any part of it, thinking it conducive to peace to avoid two jurisdictions on different parts of the same island; and in return for this forbearance the British Minister, yielding perhaps to some selfish clamor of a trading company, as much against British interests as against American rights, reproduces on an American island the inconvenience of divided occupation, which it was the very purpose of the treaty to avoid.

If the hum of the American seaboard is in part the echo of sentiments from abroad, here the unmixed voice of America may be heard, as it pronounces that it is too late to wrest territory from the United States by prevarication, by menace, or by force. From the English dockyards it is a long voyage to San Juan; the only good land route across the continent lies south of Lake Superior; in a few years there will be three Ohios on the shores of the Pacific. It is England's interest as well as duty to give effect to the treaty as it was interpreted by her own minister to ours. Your voices on this memorable day give the instruction to our own Government to abide by the treaty faithfully, on the condition that Britain will do the same; but the treaty must bind neither party or both—must be executed in good faith or canceled. The men who honor the memory of Perry will always know how to defend the domain of their country.

Has any European statesman been miscounting the strength of this nation, by substituting a reminiscence of our feeble confederation for the present efficient and almost perfect organism of the body politic? Has any foreign ruler been so foolish as to listen with credulity to the tales of impending disunion? Every man of the people of Ohio, this great central highway of national travel, will, without one exception, tell the calumniator or the unbeliever that the voices of discontent among us are but the evanescent vapor of men's breath; that our little domestic strifes are no more than momentary disturbances on the surface, easily settled among ourselves; that the love of Union has wound its cords indissolubly round the whole American people.

So, then, our last word shall be for the Union. The Union will guard the fame of its defenders, and ever more protect our entire territory; it will keep alive for mankind, the beacon lights of popular liberty and power; it will dissuade nations in a state of unripeness from attempting to found republican governments before they spring up naturally by an inward law; and its mighty heart will throb with delight at every true advance in any part of the world, toward republican happiness and freedom.

SYSTEMS OF BELIEF.
Rev. W. H. Milburn, 1860.

Pleasure is right, and right is pleasure; and hence comes the system of Epicurus. Epicurus fasted because it gave him an exquisite taste and enjoyment of his meal; Epicurus slept not unduly because with his waking he found his intellect balanced and his *physique* refreshed. He awaked and remained awake, in order that his slumber might bring him quiet and repose. Thus starting from his condition we come very naturally to the luxury of the Sybarite, where the crimson wine sparkles and obscenity riots, and where the forms of vice and beastly debauchery flourish, in the saloons, the gambling-houses, and drinking-shops of this city. In all the forms of impurity and sensuality you have the practical life of this Epicurean philosophy: virtue is pleasure; therefore, pleasure is virtue, and wherever there is wrong done to our nature, by the gratification of our animal passions; wherever God's law is degraded and man's nature reduced to the level of the brute—you have the practical exposition of the tenets of the system.

Upon the other hand, the system of Zeno seems to stand in direct opposition, in antipodal relations to that of Epicurus. Virtue sufficeth, says Zeno. Virtue is the law of the universe; the universe is law, law and law only. Dead, mechanical force, iron necessity; the sweep of fatalism in its terrific circle; this, and nothing more. No pulse of pity; no heart of tenderness; no thought of God in all the sweep of imagination or circle of reason. I, man, am a microcosm, a synopsis of all the laws and facts of the universe; I am not only part and parcel of it, but an image and reflection of it; virtue is resident in the mind, and has nothing to do with pain or pleasure. Pain and pleasure are of the senses and are wholly alien to the understanding, says Zeno. I am to be master of all suffering. What care I for infirmity? I stand here the noblest being in the whole creation; may I not be master of that creation? The brutes may writhe in their ecstasy of pain, they may shriek in the fearful spasms of their suffering; but I, a man, that seem to be a mirror of creation, may I not be master of these agonies, and stand, with folded arms, disdainful of every sort of sorrow, of all pangs of pity, or tenderness, or affection? of what is called friendship, love? These things are the whimpering sentimentalities of women and children, and I have nothing to do with them. The folded arms, the clenched fist, the tightly drawn lips, be mine; and if pain become too strong for suffering there is a portal which my own hand can open; it swings apart obedient to my poignard, and suicide is my resort; therefore apathy is the perfection of human character; a deadness of sentiment, a hardihood of courage, a noble daring, a port of pride, a disdainful mien—these are what become the intellect as the master of the earth.

SYSTEMS OF BELIEF.

Therefore, my brain is to be all crystal, my heart of adamant. Such is the Stoical system. In both there was much of beauty and ingenuity, of philosophical insight and depth, largeness of conception, fullness and admirableness of treatment. But they both, in common with all other systems, aside and apart from our holy faith, lacked one master-power; the great power of the heart, which appeals to the heart of the whole earth.

I might convince your understanding of the propriety of Epicureanism, of the grandeur and nobleness of Stoicism; I might warm you in this direction; I might chill you in that; but when I speak to that part of your nature which is deeper and nobler than the intellect; when I come to ask the suffrage of a simple human nature, I must be armed with a sublimer word than the language of either. Take Christianity in comparison with them; it teaches that there is consistency and coherency between virtue and pleasure, but that I am to be loyal to virtue. It unites the opposite systems of Epicurus and Zeno; it takes their half-truths and solidifies and unites them in one complete full-orbed and rounded whole.

THE INDIAN CHIEF.

[The following poem is founded on a traditionary story which is common on the borders of the great Falls of Niagara, although differing in some unimportant particulars.]

The rain fell in torrents, the thunder roll'd deep,
And silenced the cataract's roar;
But neither the night, nor the tempest could keep
The warrior chieftain on shore.

The war-shout has sounded, the stream must be cross'd
Why lingers the leader afar?
'Twere better his life than his glory be lost;
He never came late to the war.

He seized a canoe as he sprang from the rock,
But fast as the shore fled his reach,
The mountain wave seem'd all his efforts to mock,
And dash'd the canoe on the beach.

"Great Spirit," he cried "shall the battle be given,
And all but their leader be there?
May this struggle land me with them or in heaven!"
And he push'd with the strength of despair.

He has quitted the shore, he has gained the deep;
His guide is the lightning alone!
But he felt not with fast, irresistible sweep,
The rapids were bearing him down!

But the cataract's roar with the thunder now vied;
"Oh, what is the meaning of this?"
He spoke, and just turn'd to the cataract's side,
As the lightning flash'd down the abyss.

All the might of his arm to one effort was given,
At self-preservation's command;
But the treacherous oar with the effort was riven,
And the fragment remain'd in his hand.

"Be it so," cried the warrior, taking his seat,
And folding his bow to his breast;
"Let the cataract shroud my pale corpse with its sheet,
And its roar lull my spirit to rest.

THE INDIAN CHIEF.

"The prospect of death with the brave I have borne,
I shrink not to bear it alone;
I have often faced death when the hope was forlorn,
But I shrink not to face him with none."

The thunder was hush'd, and the battle-field stain'd,
When the sun met the war-wearied eye,
But no trace of the boat, or the chieftain remain'd,
Though his bow was still seen in the sky.

THE INDEPENDENT FARMER.

W. W. Fosdick.

Let sailors sing the windy deep,
Let soldiers praise their armor.
But in my heart this toast I'll keep,
The Independent Farmer:
When first the rose, in robe of green,
Unfolds its crimson lining,
And round his cottage porch is seen
The honeysuckle twining;
When banks of bloom their sweetness yield,
To bees that gather honey,
He drives his team across the field,
Where skies are soft and sunny.

The blackbird clucks behind his plow,
The quail pipes loud and clearly;
Yon orchard hides behind its bough
The home he loves so dearly;
The gray, old barn, whose doors enfold
His ample store in measure,
More rich than heaps of hoarded gold,
A precious, blessed treasure;
But yonder in the porch there stands
His wife, the lovely charmer,
The sweetest rose on all his lands—
The Independent Farmer.

To him the spring comes dancing gay,
To him the summer blushes;
The autumn smiles with mellow ray,
His sleep old winter hushes.
He cares not how the world may move,
No doubts or fears confound him;
His little flock are link'd in love,
And household angels round him;
He trusts in God and loves his wife,
Nor grief nor ill may harm her,
He's nature's noble man in life—

The Independent Farmer.

MRS. GRAMMAR'S BALL.

Anon.

Mrs. Grammar she gave a ball
To the nine different parts of Speech,—
To the big and the tall,
To the short and the small,
There were pies, plums, and puddings for each.

And first, little Articles came,
In a hurry to make themselves known—
Fat A, An, and The,
But none of the three
Could stand for a minute alone.

Then Adjectives came to announce
That their dear friends the Nouns were at hand.
Rough, Rougher, and Roughest,
Tough, Tougher, and Toughest,
Fat, Merry, Good-natured, and Grand.

The Nouns were, indeed, on their way—
Ten thousand and more, I should think;
For each name that we utter—
Shop, Shoulder, and Shutter—
Is a Noun: Lady, Lion, and Link.

The Pronouns were following fast
To push the Nouns out of their places,—
I, Thou, You, and Me,
We, They, He, and She,
With their merry, good-humor'd old faces.

Some cried out—"Make way for the Verbs!"
A great crowd is coming in view—
To Bite and to Smite,
And to Light and to Fight,
To Be, and to Have, and to Do.

The Adverbs attend on the Verbs,
Behind them as footmen they run;
As thus:—"To fight Badly,

MRS. GRAMMAR'S BALL.

They run away Gladly,"
Shows how fighting and running were done.

Prepositions came—In, By, and Near,
With Conjunctions, a poor little band,
As—"Either you Or me,
But Neither them Nor he"
They held their great friends by the hand.

Then, with Hip, Hip, Hurra!
Hushed Interjections uproarious—
"Oh, dear! Well-a-day!"
When they saw the display,
"Ha! ha!" they all shouted out, "Glorious!"

But, alas, what misfortunes were nigh!
While the fun and the feastings pleased each,
There pounced in at once
A monster—a Dunce,
And confounded the Nine parts of Speech!

Help, friends! to the rescue! on you
For aid Noun and Article call,—
Oh, give your protection
To poor Interjection,
Verb, Adverb, Conjunction, and all!

HOW THE MONEY COMES.

Queer John has sung, how money goes,
But how it comes, who knows? Who knows?
Why every Yankee mother's son
Can tell you how "the thing" is done.
It comes by honest toil and trade;
By wielding sledge and driving spade,
And building ships, balloons, and drums;
And that's the way the money comes.

How does it come? Why, as it goes,
By spinning, weaving, knitting hose,
By stitching shirts and coats for Jews,
Erecting churches, renting pews,
And manufacturing boots and shoes;
For thumps and twists, and cuts and hues,
And *heads* and *hearts*, tongues, lungs, and thumbs
And that's the way the money comes.

How does it come? The way is plain—
By raising cotton, corn, and *cane*;
By wind and steam, lightning and rain;
By guiding ships across the main;
By building bridges, roads, and dams,
And sweeping streets, and digging clams,
With whistles, hi's! ho's! and hums!
And that's the way the money comes.

The money comes—how did I say?
Not *always* in an *honest* way.
It comes by *trick* as well as toil,
But how is that? why, slick as oil,—
By putting peas in coffee-bags;
By swapping watches, knives, and nags,
And peddling *wooden clocks* and *plums*;
And that's the way the money comes.

How does it come?—wait, let me see,
It very seldom comes to me;
It comes by *rule* I guess, and *seale*,
Sometimes by riding on a *rail*,

HOW THE MONEY COMES.

But oftener, that's the way it goes
From silly belles and fast young beaux;
It comes in big, nay, *little sums*,
Ay! that's the way the money comes.

THE FUTURE OF THE FASHIONS.
Punch.

There was a time when girls wore hoops of steel,
And with gray powder used to drug their hair,
Bedaub'd their cheeks with rouge; white lead, or meal,
Added, to stimulate complexions fair;
Whereof by contrast to enhance the grace,
Specks of court-plaster deck'd the female face.

That fashion pass'd away, and then were worn
Dresses whose skirts came scarce below the knee,
With waists girt round the shoulder-blades, and scorn,
Now pointed at the prior finery,
When here and there some antiquated dame
Still wore it, to afford her juniors game.

Short waists departed; Taste awhile prevail'd
Till ugly Folly's reign return'd once more,
And ladies then went draggle-tail'd;
And now they wear hoops also, as before.
Paint, powder, patches, nasty and absurd,
They'd wear as well, if France had spoke the word.

Young bucks and beauties, ye who now deride
The reasonable dress of other days;
When time your forms shall have puffed out or dried,
Then on your present portraits you will gaze,
And say what dowdies, frights, and guys you were,
With their more precious figures to compare.

Think, if you live till you are lean or fat,
Your features blurred, your eyes bedimm'd with age,
Your limbs have stiffen'd; feet grown broad and flat:
You may see other garments all the rage,
Preposterous as even that attire
Which you in mirrors now so much admire.

LOYALTY TO LIBERTY OUR ONLY HOPE.
Bishop Whipple, of Minnesota.

The love of country is the gift of God—it can not dwell in homes of sin, it has no abiding place in saloons of vice or dens of infamy, it belongs not to infidel clubs or fanatical conventions, they would tear down the sacred edifice which they have never loved; they are impatient for change, for in the seething caldron of rebellion they are brought to the surface. With nothing to lose, they have no fear of the days of terror; their only dread is in the majesty of the law. The love of country belongs to a God-fearing people; it is seen in the purity of private life, in the privacy of Christian homes, in the devotions of the closet, in the manliness of Christian character. The church is its nursing mother. Loyalty to God and to His institutions is her first and last lesson; it is the earnest cry of her loyal children "that peace and happiness, truth and justice, religion and piety may be established among us for all generations." The love of country belongs to loyal men. The power of self-government depends upon a loyal people.

The protection of the nation depends not on the wisdom of its senators, not on the vigilance of its police, not on the strong arm of standing armies: but the loyalty of a united people. Other nations have equaled us in all the arts of civilization, in discoveries, in science, in skill, and in invention; they have kept even step with us and often surpassed us in philosophy and literature; they have been brave in war and wise in council; they have clustered around their homes all that art can lavish of beauty—but ripe scholarship, cunning in art, or skill in invention, never gave to the people a constitution. This is the outgrowth of a manly spirit of loyalty. It teaches men *duty*—a right manly word for right manly men. Loyalty was God's gift to our fathers; it was learned in the hard school of adversity, and by self-denial and suffering inwrought into the nation's life; it grew up in the sheltered valleys and on the rocky hillsides of New England, it was cradled in Virginia, in New York, in the Carolinas, among the patricians of Virginia; it gave to the world a Washington, and from the shop, the store, the farm, and professional life there sprung up from the people many who shared his spirit to become the founders of the Republic.

OUR COUNTRY FIRST, LAST, AND ALWAYS.
Ibid.

The first defense to any people is in the love of country. The nation is one great family, with one common interest, welfare, and destiny; a nation dwelling together in love must be a happy people. Kindness begets kindness, and love awakens love; this is that magic touch which makes the world of kin. A confederacy like ours can not be held together by the strong arm of a central government; if the band of unity is gone, such a union is no whit better than a rope of sand. The danger which besets us is not in individual sins which fasten on the body politic—we may labor with forbearance and firmness for their removal. Our danger lies in that spirit of selfishness and self-will which forgets brotherhood and God. In a nation like ours, with its countless differing interests of rival productions, its conflicts of trade and sectional rivalries of commerce, we must differ on questions of public policy; but it may be the manly difference of manly men. Never did men differ more widely than the fathers of the republic, never did earnest hearts battle with more zeal for their rival interests, nor contend more fiercely inch by inch in political struggles. Never did the rallying cry of parties take a deeper hold on its liege-men, or braver shouts of triumph herald in its victory. But there was a deeper love of country, which made the brotherhood of a nation, and a charity which more respected the opinions of those from whom they differ. The Christian patriot dare not close his eye to the evils which mar the nation; for their removal he will work and pray, but never with rash hand tear down the sacred edifice of the Constitution, because some stains deface its walls. The query may well arise whether we are not fast reaching the time when the question is not of the right or wrong of this or that legislation, the benefit of this or that public policy, but whether this or that party shall divide the spoils of office among their political camp followers. We hear of angry words and fierce invectives, of rumors of corruption, of bribery in public office; they belong to no one party, they are not ranked under any one leader; these things came because the people have lost sight, in the strifes of men for office, of that great destiny which God offers to Americans. I believe the love of country dwells in the people's hearts. The honest-hearted sons of toil will be true to the country and its constitution. That love may have slumbered for a time, but the great heart of the country *will* be true to itself. Its love *can not* be hedged in by the paling of any man's door-yard. It *will* sweep away every barrier of strife, and keep us one united people.

BRITISH INFLUENCE.

John Randolph.

Imputations of British influence have been uttered against the opponents of this war. Against whom are these charges brought? Against men who, in the war of the Revolution, were in the Councils of the Nation, or fighting the battles of your country! And by whom are these charges made? By runaways, chiefly from the British dominions, since the breaking out of the French troubles. The great autocrat of all the Russias receives the homage of our high consideration. The Dey of Algiers and his divan of pirates are very civil, good sort of people, with whom we find no difficulty in maintaining the relations of peace and amity. "Turks, Jews, and Infidels,"—Melimelli or the Little Turtle,—barbarians and savages of every clime and color, are welcome to our arms. With chiefs of banditti, negro or mulatto, we can treat and can trade. Name, however, but England, and all our antipathies are up in arms against her. Against whom? Against those whose blood runs in our veins; in common with whom we claim Shakspeare, and Newton, and Chatham, for our countrymen; whose form of government is the freest on earth, our own only excepted; from whom every valuable principle of our own institutions has been borrowed,—representation, jury trial, voting the supplies, writ of habeas corpus, our whole civil and criminal jurisprudence;—against our fellow-Protestants, identified in blood, in language, in religion, with ourselves.

In what school did the worthies of our land—the Washingtons, Henrys, Hancocks, Franklins, Rutledges, of America—learn those principles of civil liberty which were so nobly asserted by their wisdom and valor? American resistance to British usurpation has not been more warmly cherished by these great men and their compatriots,—not more by Washington, Hancock, and Henry,—than by Chatham, and his illustrious associates in the British Parliament. It ought to be remembered, too, that the heart of the English people was with us. It was a selfish and corrupt ministry, and their servile tools, to whom *we* were not more opposed than *they* were. I trust that none such may ever exist among us; for tools will never be wanting to subserve the purposes, however ruinous or wicked, of kings and ministers of state. I acknowledge the influence of a Shakspeare and a Milton upon my imagination; of a Locke, upon my understanding; of a Sidney, upon my political principles; of a Chatham, upon qualities which would to God I possessed in common with that illustrious man! of a Tillotson, a Sherlock, and a Porteus, upon my religion. This is a British influence which I can never shake off.

DEFENSE OF THOMAS JEFFERSON.
Henry Clay.

Next to the notice which the opposition has found itself called upon to bestow upon the French emperor, a distinguished citizen of Virginia, formerly President of the United States, has never for a moment failed to receive their kindest and most respectful attention. An honorable gentleman from Massachusetts, of whom I am sorry to say, it becomes necessary for me, in the course of my remarks, to take some notice, has alluded to him in a remarkable manner. Neither his retirement from public office, his eminent services, nor his advanced age, can exempt this patriot from the coarse assaults of party malevolence. No, sir! In 1801, he snatched from the rude hand of usurpation the violated Constitution of his country,—and *that* is his crime. He preserved that instrument, in form, and substance, and spirit, a precious inheritance for generations to come,—and for *this* he can never be forgiven. How vain and impotent is party rage, directed against such a man! He is not more elevated by his lofty residence, upon the summit of his own favorite mountain, than he is lifted, by the serenity of his mind and the consciousness of a well-spent life, above the malignant passions and bitter feelings of the day. No! his own beloved Monticello is not less moved by the storms that beat against its sides, than is this illustrious man, by the howlings of the whole British pack, let loose from the Essex kennel! When the gentleman to whom I have been compelled to allude shall have mingled his dust with that of his abused ancestors,—when he shall have been consigned to oblivion, or, if he lives at all, shall live only in the treasonable annals of a certain junto,—the name of Jefferson will be hailed with gratitude, his memory honored and cherished as the second founder of the liberties of the people, and the period of his administration will be looked back to as one of the happiest and brightest epochs of American history!

NATIONAL HATREDS ARE BARBAROUS.
Rufus Choate.

That there exists in this country an intense sentiment of nationality; a cherished energetic feeling and consciousness of our independent and separate national existence; a feeling that we have a transcendent destiny to fulfil, which we mean to fulfil; a great work to do, which we know how to do, and are able to do; a career to run, up which we hope to ascend, till we stand on the steadfast and glittering summits of the world; a feeling, that we are surrounded and attended by a noble historical group of competitors and rivals, the other nations of the earth, all of whom we hope to overtake, and even to distance;—such a sentiment as this exists, perhaps, in the character of this people. And this I do not discourage, I do not condemn. But, sir, that among these useful and beautiful sentiments, predominant among them, there exists a temper of hostility towards this one particular nation, to such a degree as to amount to a habit, a trait, a national passion,—to amount to a state of feeling which "is to be regretted," and which really threatens another war,—this I earnestly and confidently deny. I would not hear your enemy say this. Sir, the indulgence of such a sentiment by the people supposes them to have forgotten one of the counsels of Washington. Call to mind the ever seasonable wisdom of the Farewell Address: "The nation which indulges toward another an habitual hatred, or an habitual fondness, is, in some degree, a slave. It is a slave to its animosity, or to its affection, either of which is sufficient to lead it astray from its duty and its interest."

No, sir! no, sir! We are above all this. Let the Highland clansman, half-naked, half-civilized, half-blinded by the peat-smoke of his cavern, have his hereditary enemy and his hereditary enmity, and keep the keen, deep, and precious hatred, set on fire of hell, alive, if he can; let the North American Indian have his, and hand it down from father to son, by Heaven knows what symbols of alligators, and rattlesnakes, and war-clubs smeared with vermilion and entwined with scarlet; let such a country as Poland,—cloven to the earth, the armed heel on the radiant forehead, her body dead, her soul incapable to die,—let her remember the "wrongs of days long past;" let the lost and wandering tribes of Israel remember theirs—the manliness and the sympathy of the world may allow or pardon this to them;—but shall America, young, free, prosperous, just setting out on the highway of heaven, "decorating and cheering the elevated sphere she just begins to move in, glittering like the morning star, full of life and joy," shall she be supposed to be polluting and corroding her noble and happy heart, by moping over old stories of stamp act, and tea tax, and the firing of the Leopard upon the Chesapeake in a time of peace?

No, sir! no, sir! a thousand times, no! Why, I protest I thought all that had been settled. I thought two wars had settled it all. What else was so much good blood shed for, on so many more than classical fields of Revolutionary glory? For what was so much good blood more lately shed, at Lundy's Lane, at Fort Erie, before and behind the lines at New Orleans, on the deck of the Constitution, on the deck of the Java, on the lakes, on the sea, but to settle exactly these "wrongs of past days?" And have we come back sulky and sullen from the very field of honor? For my country, I deny it.

MURDER WILL OUT.
Daniel Webster.

An aged man, without an enemy in the world, in his own house, and in his own bed, is made the victim of a butcherly murder, for mere pay. The fatal blow is given! and the victim passes, without a struggle or a motion, from the repose of sleep to the repose of death! It is the assassin's purpose to make sure work. He explores the wrist for the pulse. He feels for it, and ascertains that it beats no longer! It is accomplished. The deed is done. He retreats, retraces his steps to the window, passes out through it as he came in, and escapes. He has done the murder;—no eye has seen him, no ear has heard him. The *secret* is his own,—and it is safe!

Ah! gentlemen, that was a dreadful mistake. Such a secret can be safe nowhere. The whole creation of God has neither nook nor corner where the guilty can bestow it, and say it is safe. Not to speak of that eye which glances through all disguises, and beholds every thing as in the splendor of noon, such secrets of guilt are never safe from detection, even by men. True it is, generally speaking, that "murder will out." True it is, that Providence hath so ordained, and doth so govern things, that those who break the great law of heaven, by shedding man's blood, seldom succeed in avoiding discovery. Especially, in a case exciting so much attention as this, discovery must come, and will come, sooner or later. A thousand eyes turn at once to explore every man, every thing, every circumstance, connected with the time and place; a thousand ears catch every whisper; a thousand excited minds intensely dwell on the scene, shedding all their light, and ready to kindle the slightest circumstance into a blaze of discovery. Meantime, the guilty soul can not keep its own secret. It is false to itself; or, rather, it feels an irresistible impulse of conscience to be true to itself. It labors under its guilty possession, and knows not what to do with it. The human heart was not made for the residence of such an inhabitant. It finds itself preyed on by a torment, which it dares not acknowledge to God nor man. A vulture is devouring it, and it can ask no sympathy or assistance, either from heaven or earth. The secret which the murderer possesses soon comes to possess him; and, like the evil spirits of which we read, it overcomes him, and leads him whithersoever it will. He feels it beating at his heart, rising to his throat, and demanding disclosure. He thinks the whole world sees it in his face, reads it in his eyes, and almost hears its workings in the very silence of his thoughts. It has become his master. It betrays his discretion, it breaks down his courage, it conquers his prudence. When suspicions from without, begin to embarrass him, and the net of circumstance to entangle him, the fatal secret struggles, with still greater violence, to burst forth. It *must* be confessed;—it *will* be confessed;—there is no refuge from confession but suicide—and suicide is confession!

STRIVE FOR THE BEST.

'Tis better to give a kindly word
Than ever so hard a blow,
To know we have by kindness stirr'd
The man who was our foe;
To feel we have a good intent,
Whatever he may feel—
That gentleness with us is meant
To make the old wounds heal.

'Tis better to give our wealth away
Than let our neighbors want,
To help them in their needful day,
While they are weak and gaunt;
A kindly deed brings kindly thought
In hamlet and in city;
A little help, we have been taught,
Is worth a world of pity.

'Tis better to work and slave and toil,
Than lie about and rust;
An idle man upon the soil
Is one of the very worst.
He eats the bread that others earn,
And lifts his head so high,
As if it was not his concern
How others toil'd, or why.

'Tis better to have an humble heart,
Living in faith and trust,
To act an ever upward part,
Remembering we are dust;
To let the streams of life run past,
Beloved and lovingly,
Until we reach in joy at last
The great eternal sea.

EARLY RISING.

John G. Saxe.

"God bless the man who first invented sleep!"
So Sancho Panza said, and so say I;
And bless him, also, that he didn't keep
His great discovery to himself; or try
To make it—as the lucky fellow might—
A close monopoly by "patent right!"

Yes—bless the man who first invented sleep
(I really can't avoid the iteration);
But blast the man, with curses loud and deep,
Whate'er the rascal's name, or age, or station,
Who first invented, and went round advising
That artificial cut-off—Early Rising!

"Rise with the lark, and with the lark to bed,"
Observes some solemn, sentimental owl.
Maxims like these are very cheaply said;
But ere you make yourself a fool or fowl,
Pray, just inquire about the rise—and fall,
And whether larks have any bed at all!

The "time for honest folks to be in bed,"
Is in the morning, if I reason right;
And he who can not keep his precious head
Upon his pillow till 'tis fairly light,
And so enjoys his forty morning winks,
Is up to knavery; or else—he drinks!

Thomson, who sung about the "Seasons," said
It was a glorious thing to *rise* in season;
But then he said it—lying—in his bed
At 10 o'clock, A. M.—the very reason
He wrote so charmingly. The simple fact is,
His preaching wasn't sanctioned by his practice.

'Tis, doubtless, well to be sometimes awake—
Awake to duty and awake to truth—
But when, alas! a nice review we take
Of our best deeds and days, we find, in sooth,

EARLY RISING.

The hours that leave the slightest cause to weep,
Are those we pass'd in childhood, or—asleep!

'Tis beautiful to leave the world awhile,
For the soft visions of the gentle night;
And free at last from mortal care or guile,
To live, as only in the angels' sight,
In sleep's sweet realms so cosily shut in,
Where, at the worst, we only *dream* of sin!

So, let us sleep, and give the Maker praise.
I like the lad who, when his father thought
To clip his morning nap by hackney'd phrase
Of vagrant worm by early songster caught,
Cried: "Served him right! it's not at all surprising—
The worm was punish'd, sir, for early rising!"

DEEDS OF KINDNESS.

Suppose the little cowslip
Should hang its golden cup,
And say: "I'm such a tiny flower,
I'd better not grow up;"
How many a weary traveler
Would miss its fragrant smell!
How many a little child would grieve
To lose it from the dell!

Suppose the glistening dew-drops
Upon the grass should say:
"What can a little dew-drop do?
I'd better roll away;"
The blade on which it rested,
Before the day was done,
Without a drop to moisten it,
Would wither in the sun.

Suppose the little breezes,
Upon a summer's day,
Should think themselves too small to cool
The traveler on his way;
Who would not miss the smallest
And softest ones that blow,
And think they made a great mistake
If they were talking so?

How many deeds of kindness
A little child may do,
Although it has so little strength,
And little wisdom, too!
It wants a loving spirit
Much more than strength, to prove
How many things a child may do
For others by his love.

THE GATES OF SLEEP.

Dr. John Henry.

There are two gates of Sleep, the poet says:
Of polished ivory one, of horn the other;
But I, besides these gates, to blessed Sleep
Three other gates have found which thus I count:
First the star-spangled arch of deep midnight,
When labor ceases, every sound is hush'd,
And Nature, drowsy, nods upon her throne.
Pale-visaged Specters round this gate keep watch,
And Fears and Horrors vain, and beyond these
Rest, balmy Sweat, and dim Forgetfulness,
Relieved, at dawn of day, by buoyant Hope,
Fresh Strength and ruddy Health and calm Composure
And daring Enterprise and Self-reliance.

The second gate is wreathed, sideposts and lintel,
With odorous trailing hop, and poppy-stalks;
The shadowy gateway paved with poppy-heads,
And there, all day and night, keeps watch sick Fancy
Haggard and trembling, and Delirium wild,
And Impotence with drunken glistening eye,
And Idiocy, and, in the background, Death.

The third gate is of lead, and there sits, ever
Humming her tedious tune, Monotony,
Tired of herself; about her on the ground
Sermons and psalms and hymns lie numerous strew'd,
To the same import all, and all almost
In the same words varied in form and order
To cheat, if possible, the weary sense,
And different seem, where difference is none.
At th' opposite doorpost, on her knees, Routine
Keeps turning over still the well-thumbed leaves
Of the same prayer-book, reading prayers, not praying;
Behind them waiting stand Conformity
And Uniformity, Oneness of faith,
Oneness of laws and customs, arts and manners,
And Self-development's unrelenting foe,

Centralization; and behind these still,
Far in the portal's deepest gloom ensconced,
A perfect, unimprovable Paradise
Of mere, blank naught, unchangeable forever—
These, as *I* count them, are the Gates of Sleep.

THE BUGLE.
Tennyson.

The splendor falls on castle walls,
And snowy summits old in story;
The long light shines across the lake,
And the wild cataract leaps in glory.
Blow, bugle, blow, set the wild echoes flying;
Blow, bugle; answer, echoes, dying, dying, dying.

Oh, hark! oh, hear! how thin and clear,
And thinner, clearer, farther going;
Oh, sweet and far, from cliff and spar,
The horns of Elf-land faintly blowing.
Blow, let us hear the purple glens replying;
Blow, bugle; answer, echoes, dying, dying, dying.

Oh, love, they die in yon rich sky;
They faint on field, or hill, or river;
Our echoes roll from soul to soul,
And grow forever and forever.
Blow, bugle, blow, set the wild echoes flying
And answer, echoes, answer, dying, dying, dying.

A HOODISH GEM.

The little snarling, caroling "babies,"
That break our nightly rest,
Should be packed off to "Baby"-lon,
To "Lapland," or to "Brest."

From "Spit"-head, "Cooks" go o'er to "Greece,"
And while the "Miser" waits
His passage to the "Guinea" coast,
"Spendthrifts" are in the "Straits."

"Spinsters" should to the "Needles" go,
"Wine-bibbers" to "Burgundy;"
"Gourmands" should lunch at "Sandwich Isles,"
"Wags" at the Bay of "Fun"-dy.

"Bachelors" flee to the "United States,"
"Maids" to the "Isle of Man;"
Let "Gardeners" go to "Botany" Bay,
And "Shoe-blacks" to "Japan."

Thus emigrate, and misplaced men
Will they no longer vex us;
And all who ain't provided for
Had better go to "Texas."

PURITY OF THE AMERICAN STRUGGLE.
By Hon. Henry Wilson. 1859.

While the exalted heroism of the illustrious men who, in the Cabinet and field, defied and baffled the whole power of the British empire, excites the admiration of mankind, the consciousness that the founders of American Independence were not allured into that deadly struggle by the lust of dominion and power, by the seductions of interest and ambition, or by the dazzling dreams of glory and renown, excites far higher and holier emotions. Theirs was not a contest of interest, of ambition or of glory,—theirs was a contest for principle, for the inherent and indefeasible rights of humanity. They accepted the bloody issues of civil war, rather than surrender the liberties of the people. When the terrific struggle began, which was not to be closed until the power of England on the North American continent was broken, they reverently "appealed to the supreme Ruler of the universe for the rectitude of their intentions;" and when it closed with the Independence of America achieved, they avowed to mankind in the sincerity of profound conviction that they "had contended for the rights of human nature." They "deduced from universal principles," in the words of the brilliant and philosophic Bancroft, "a bill of rights as old as creation and as wide as humanity." They embodied in this bill of rights, the promulgation of which made this day immortal in history, these sublime ideas: "all men are created equal;" "endowed by their creator with the inalienable rights to life, liberty, and the pursuit of happiness;" "to secure these rights, governments are instituted among men, deriving their just powers from the consent of the governed;" and "whenever any form of government becomes destructive of these ends, it is the right of the people to alter or abolish it." The embodiment of these ideas, these self-evident truths, which "are as old as creation, and as wide as humanity," into the organic law of Independent America, associated the names of the founders of national independence with the general cause of human liberty, development and progress. They were champions of American Independence,—they were, also, the champions of the sacred rights of human nature, and mankind proudly claims them, in the words of Mirabeau, "as the heroes of humanity."

OLD AGE.
Theodore Parker.

The old man loves the sunshine and fire—the arm-chair and the shady nook. A rude wind would jostle the full-grown apple from its bough, full ripe, full colored, too. The internal characteristics correspond. General activity is less. Salient love of new things and of persons, which hit the young man's heart, fades away. He thinks the old is better. He is not venturesome; he keeps at home. Passion once stung him into quickened life; now, that gadfly is no more buzzing in his ears.

Madame de Stael finds compensation in silence for the decay of the passion that once fired her blood; heathen Socrates, seventy years old, thanks the gods that he is now free from that "ravenous beast" which has disturbed his philosophic meditations for many years. Romance is the child of passion and imagination—the sudden father that, the long-protracting mother this. Old age has little romance. Only some rare man, like Wilhelm Von Humboldt, keeps it still fresh in his bosom.

In intellectual matters, the old man loves to recall the old time, to review his favorite old men—no new ones half so fair. So in Homer, Nestor, who is the oldest of the Greeks, is always talking of the olden times, before the grandfathers of the men then living had come into being; "not such as living had degenerate days." Verse-loving John Quincy Adams turns off from Byron and Shelley, and Wieland and Goethe, and returns to Pope. * * * Elder Brewster expects to hear St. Martin's and Old Hundred chanted in heaven. To him heaven comes in the long-used musical tradition.

The middle-aged man looks around at the present; he hopes less and works more. The old man looks back on the field he has trod: "this is the tree I planted—this is my footstep;" and he loves his old home, his old carriage, cat, dog, staff and friend.

In lands where the vine grows, I have seen an old man sit all day long, a sunny Autumn day, before his cottage-door, in a great arm-chair, his old dog lay couched at his feet, in the genial sun. The autumn winds played in the old man's venerable hairs. Above him on the wall, purpling in the sunlight, hung the full clusters of the grapes, ripening and maturing yet more. The two were just alike—the wind stirred the vine-leaves and they fell, stirred the old man's hairs and they whitened yet more—both were waiting for the spirit in them to be fully ripe.

The young man looks forward—the old man looks back. How long the shadows lie in the setting sun—the steeples, a mile long, reaching across the plain, as the sun stretches out the hills in grotesque dimensions! So are the events of life in the old man's consciousness.

BEAUTIFUL, AND AS TRUE AS BEAUTIFUL.

[Paul Denton, a celebrated itinerant Methodist preacher and missionary, in the early days of Texas, when the State, then a Mexican province, was the outlaw's home, collected a large crowd at a barbecue where he promised there should be plenty to drink of the best of liquors. Denton did this to collect a crowd that he might preach to them. After the barbecue was over, one of the boldest told Paul that he lied. "Where is your liquor?" said he. Drawing himself up to his full height, Paul thus broke forth in a strain that remains unsurpassed:]

"There—there is the liquor which God, the Eternal, brews for his children.

"Not in the simmering still, over smoking fires choked with poisonous gases, and surrounded with stench of sickening odors and rank corruption doth your Father in Heaven prepare that precious essence of life, pure cold water. Both in the green shade and grassy dell, where the red deer wanders and the child loves to play, there God brews it; and down, low down in the deepest valleys, where the fountains murmur and the rills sing; and high up on the mountain tops, where the naked granite glitters like gold in the sun; where hurricanes howl music; where big waves roar the chorus, sweeping the march of God—there, he brews it, that beverage of life, health-giving water.

"And everywhere it is a thing of beauty; gleaming in a dew-drop; singing in the summer rain, shining in the ice-gem, till the trees seem turning to living jewels, spreading a golden vail over the setting sun; or white gauze round the midnight moon; sporting in the glacier; dancing in the hail-shower; folding bright snowy curtains softly above the wintry world, and weaving the many-colored iris, that seraph's zone of the sky, whose warp is the rain of earth, whose woof is the sunbeam of heaven, all checkered o'er with celestial flowers by the mystic hand of refraction—still always beautiful; that blessed cold water. No poison bubbles on its brink; its foam brings not madness and murder; no blood stains its liquid glass; pale widows and starving orphans weep not burning tears in its clear depths; no drunkard's shrieking from the grave curses it in words of despair! Speak out, my friends, would you exchange it for the demon's drink, alcohol?"

THE DELUGE.

The judgment was at hand. Before the sun
Gathered tempestuous clouds, which, blackening, spread
Until their blended masses overwhelmed
The hemisphere of day: and, adding gloom
To night's dark empire, swept from zone to zone—
Swept the vast shadow, swallowing up all light,
And covering the encircled firmament
As with a mighty pall! Low in the dust
Bowed the affrighted nations, worshiping.

Anon the o'ercharged garners of the storm
Burst with their growing burden; fierce and fast
Shot down the ponderous rain, a sheeted good,
That slanted not before the baffled winds,
But, with an arrowy and unwavering rush,
Dashed hissing earthward. Soon the rivers rose,
And roaring fled their channels; and calm lakes
Awoke exulting from their lethargy,
And poured destruction on their peaceful shores.

The lightning flickered in the deluged air,
And feebly through the shout of gathering waves
Muttered the stifled thunder. Day nor night
Ceased the descending streams; and if the gloom
A little brightened when the lurid morn
Rose on the starless midnight, 'twas to show
The lifting up of waters. Bird and beast
Forsook the flooded plains, and wearily
The shivering multitudes of human doomed
Toiled up before the insatiate element.

Oceans were blent, and the leviathan
Was borne aloft on the ascending seas
To where the eagles nestled. Mountains now
Were the sole landmarks, and their sides were clothed
With clustering myriads, from the weltering waste
Whose surges clasped them, to their topmost peaks
Swathed in the stooping cloud. The hand of Death
Smote millions as they climbed; yet denser grew

The crowded nations, as the encroaching waves
Narrowed their little world.
And in that hour,
Did no man aid his fellow. Love of life
Was the sole instinct; and the strong-limbed son,
With imprecations smote the palsied sire
That clung to him for succor. Women trod
With wavering steps the precipice's brow,
And found no arm to grasp on the dread verge
O'er which she leaned and trembled. Selfishness
Sat like an incubus on every heart,
Smothering the voice of Love. The giant's foot
Was on the stripling's neck: and oft despair
Grappled the ready steel, and kindred blood
Polluted the last remnant of that earth
Which God was deluging to purify.
Huge monsters from the plains, whose skeletons
The mildew of succeeding centuries
Has failed to crumble, with unwieldy strength
Crushed through the solid crowds; and fiercest birds,
Beat downward by the ever-rushing rain,
With blinded eyes, drenched plumes, and trailing wings,
Staggered unconscious o'er the trampled prey.

THE WORM OF THE STILL.

I have found what the learned seemed so puzzled to tell—
The true shape of the Devil, and where is his Hell;
Into serpents, of old, crept the Author of Ill,
But Satan works now as a worm of the still.
Of all his migrations, this last he likes best:
How the arrogant reptile here raises his crest!
His head winding up from the tail of his plan,
Till the worm stands erect o'er the prostrated man.

Here, he joys to transform, by his magical spell,
The sweet milk of the Earth to an Essence of Hell;
Fermented our food, and corrupted our grain,
To famish the stomach and madden the brain.
By his water of life, what distraction and fear;
By the gloom of its light, what pale spectres appear!
A Demon keeps time on his fiddle finance,
While his Passions spring up in a horrible dance!

Then prone on the earth, they adore in the dust,
A man's baser half, raised, in room of his bust.
Such orgies the nights of the drunkard display,
But how black with ennui, how benighted his day!
With drams it begins, and with drams must it end;
A dram is his country, his mistress, his friend;
Till the ossified heart hates itself at the last,
And the dram nerves his hand for a death-doing blast.

Mark that monster, that mother, that shame and that curse;
See the child hang dead-drunk at the breast of its nurse!
As it drops from her arm, mark her stupefied stare!
Then she wakes with a yell, and a shriek of despair.
Drink, Erin! drink deep from this crystalline round,
Till the tortures of self-recollection be drowned;
Till the hopes of thy heart be all stiffened to stone—
Then sit down in the dirt like a queen on her throne.

No phrensy for Freedom to flash o'er the brain;
Thou shalt dance to the musical clank of the chain;
A crown of cheap straw shall seem rich to thine eye
And peace and good order shall reign in the sky!

Nor boast that no track of the viper is seen,
To stain thy pure surface of Emerald green:
For the Serpent will never want poison to kill,
While the fat of your fields feeds the worm of the still!

MAN'S CONNECTION WITH THE INFINITE.

That is to every thing created pre-eminently useful, which enables it rightly and fully to perform the functions appointed to it by its Creator. Therefore, that we may determine what is chiefly useful to man, it is necessary first to determine the use of man himself.

Man's use and function is to be the witness of the glory of God, and to advance that glory by his reasonable obedience and resultant happiness.

Whatever enables us to fulfill this function is, in the pure and first sense of the word, useful to us. Pre-eminently, therefore, what sets the glory of God more brightly before us. But things that only help us to exist are, in a secondary and mean sense, useful, or rather, if they be looked for alone, they are useless and worse, for it would be better that we should not exist, than that we should guiltily disappoint the purposes of existence.

And yet people speak in this working age, when they speak from their hearts, as if houses, and lands, and food, and raiment were alone useful; and as if sight, thought, and admiration were all profitless, so that men insolently call themselves Utilitarians, who would turn, if they had their way, themselves and their race into vegetables: men who think that the meat is more than the life, and the raiment than the body; who look to the earth as a stable, and to its fruit as fodder; vine-dressers as husbandmen, who love the corn they grind, and the grapes they crush, better than the gardens of the angels upon the slopes of Eden; hewers of wood and drawers of water, who think that the wood they hew and the water they draw, are better than the pine forests that cover the mountains like the shadow of God, and than the great rivers that move like his eternity. And so comes upon us that woe of the preacher, that, though God "hath made every thing beautiful in his time, also he hath set the world in their hearts, so that no man can find out the work that God maketh from the beginning to the end."

This Nebuchadnezzar curse, that sends us to grass like oxen, seems to follow but too closely on the excess or continuance of national power and peace. In the perplexities of nations, in their struggles for existence, in their infancy, their impotence, or even their disorganization, they have higher hopes and nobler passions. Out of the suffering comes the serious mind; out of the salvation, the grateful heart; out of the endurance, the fortitude; out of the deliverance, the faith; but now, when they have learned to live under providence of laws, and with decency and justice and regard for each other, and when they have done away with violent and external sources of suffering, worse evils seem rising out of their rest—evils that vex less and mortify more, that suck the blood though they do not shed it, and ossify the heart though they do not torture it. And deep though the causes of thankfulness must be to every people at peace with others and at unity in itself, there are causes of fear also, a fear greater than the sword and sedition: that dependence on God may be forgotten, because the bread is given and the water is sure; that gratitude to him may cease, because his constancy of protection has taken the semblance of a natural law; that heavenly hope may grow faint amidst the full fruition of the world; that selfishness may take place of undemanded devotion, compassion be lost in vainglory, and love in dissimulation; that innovation may succeed to strength, apathy to patience, and the noise of jesting words and foulness of dark thoughts, to the earnest purity of the girded loins and the burning lamp.—*Ruskin.*

THE LANGUAGE OF THE EAGLE.

It is one of the difficulties of those who undertake to make public speeches, that sometimes they are embarrassed about the heads of their discourses; and so I am somewhat troubled at finding the inferior position of the American eagle, inasmuch as he has but one head, while the Russian eagle has two. I suppose that the explanation of this ornithological difference arises from the necessity of the Russian eagle having one head to watch over his large possessions in Asia, and the other head to look after his small property in Europe. I feel a good deal of confidence in speaking of the American eagle in contrast. I can see that if the American eagle has but one head, it embodies therein the national sentiment now prevailing, of one country and one people. It is very true that our brethren of the South—for I still call them our brethren—have been under the impression that ours was a double-headed eagle, with a Northern and a Southern head, with this distinction over the Russian; that the Southern was the larger and more important head of the two, and we are now engaged in the somewhat expensive and troublesome task of correcting that mistake in natural history. There is a good deal that is appropriate, and sometimes something that is suggestive, in these national symbols. The lion, for instance, is a very hungry beast, and the large portion of the globe which he has got into his possession shows the appropriateness of the selection of the symbol. The cock, as we know, is a very boisterous and demonstrative bird, who never does anything that he does not make a noise about. And certainly the Gallic neighbor of the English lion has never been distinguished for his modesty whenever he has accomplished any thing in arts or in arms. The eagle is a high-soaring bird, and I had better bring before you what an English poet says of him:

> He clasps the crag with hooked hands,
> Close to the sun in lonely lands,
> Ringed in an azure world he stands;
> The wrinkled sea beneath him crawls,
> He watches from his mountain walls,
> And like a thunderbolt he falls.

If the illustration had been carried further we might be content with this English authority that the eagle, as typical of Russia and of the United States, is to be armed with that thunderbolt which the Greeks thought to be the prerogative of Jupiter. The American eagle has been distinguished for the quickness of his flight; and I do not think that our bitterest enemies can ever bring against us the charge of slowness. There are some points of resemblance between the United States and Russia. Russia, like us, is made up of many nationalities: and we have had recently the most satisfactory evidence that the Russian eagle is soaring in the same quarter as we are—soaring beyond the crowing of the cock or the roaring of the lion.

In conclusion, the eagle was an old symbol. The Egyptians had it; the Persians had it; the Romans, after trying four or five other animals, took it, in the time, I think, of Marius. Therefore, as it is one of the oldest illustrations of national importance, I indulge in the sentiment that, as the eagle now represents the nations of Russia and the United States, it may at least be one among the latest.—*Judge Daly, of New York.*

WASHINGTON.
S. S. Cox.

All over the world examples may be found which are lessons to us. Could you go to Naples, you will find beyond the Grotto of Phisillippo, where the soft waves of the delightful Bay make their music on the shore—the tomb of the great Latin poet—Virgil. Men from every clime go thither to pay their homage to his tomb, although two thousand years have gone since his Epic was given to the world. His tomb is still the mausoleum of Genius. It is respected, protected and honored. Some of you have seen the monuments Scotland has reared to her gifted men. Some of you have seen the tomb of Walter Scott, at Dryburg Abbey, and have not only admired its beauty and repose, but have admired the vigilant care with which it is guarded and protected.

Go to Rome! Beneath St. Peter's Bascilica, you will find there the tombs of the Apostles Peter and Paul. They are guarded ever by priestly vigilance, and around them burn the ever-trimmed lamps of religious veneration. At Paris, the great Napoleon sleeps, honored in death beyond all human conquerors, in the *Hotel des Invalides*, surrounded by a hundred banners, emblems of his victories and his genius!

England has her Westminster Hall, wherein is enshrined her royal line, and by a higher heritage a line of genius, from Chaucer, who sung the dawn of English verse, to Macaulay, who illustrated her history in the undying eloquence of his prose. France has her St. Denis, the last abode of her kings, and Paris has its Pantheon, in whose vaults the literary demigods are immortalized!

But I pass these reminiscences by. We have a tomb which, I trust, in future, will be cared for and protected; and as long as woman is the watcher, her faith and patience will guard it with vestal vigilance.

It is neither a trite nor an untrue saying, that if a man bears the blade of patriotism, woman is the jewel in its hilt. She has and ever will make that jewel shine, wherever there is a fair opportunity and an ennobling civilization.

Why has this association of American women been formed? For the purpose of purchasing, preserving, reclaiming and protecting that spot we have just left, so sacred in our historic annals and in the nation's memory. It is because the man who lies there buried is not the mere hero of a novel—not the mere hero of to-day—not the mere soldier who achieved with his own sword his own fortune—not your Sultan Mohammed or Emperor Napoleon, who, with bloody ambition, created an empire on the Bosphorus or a dynasty on the Seine. The career of these heroes of the battle-field is as yonder blood-red moon, just risen above the Potomac, compared with the bright effulgence of the noonday sun, which shines with no borrowed light, as an auriole around the memory of George Washington. He can be addressed at this day, when he is so canonized in our hearts, only in the language of that poetry which has likened him to the brightest imagery which the material universe can furnish. He has been spoken of as the illustrious but lost Pleiad in our American constellation.

AMERICA VS. ENGLAND.
David Dudley Field.

It has been said that if a new dictionary were now to be published in England, another definition of neutrality would have to be given. Certain it is that much of what has taken place on the other side of the ocean during this unhappy war comports little with our previous understanding of the duties of neutrals. And yet strict neutrality between belligerents is enjoined as much by philanthropy as by national honor; for while it protects national independence it restricts the limits of war. It is thus a rule alike of justice and of prudence. It springs from principles which lie at the foundation of international law; that is to say, the independence and the equality of nations. But there is another rule which springs from the same principles, and which is as old and as strong as that of neutrality, and is sometimes confounded with it—that is, the duty of every nation to abstain from any interference with the internal concerns of another. To be neutral between two belligerents is to help neither; to make, or help to make, two belligerents out of the same nation is to interfere in its internal relations. If it be said that this is but to recognize and declare a fact, I answer that the nation itself, as it is equal and independent, is the sole judge of the fact. The relation of the different parts with each other is a domestic concern. To assume to recognize and declare relations which it does not first recognize and declare, is, equally with the violation of neutrality, a departure from that courtesy and deference which are due from one nation to another. Both depend upon that public law of the world which is as old as governments and as eternal as equity. No nation is so ancient or mighty as to be above it; none so young or weak as to be below it. Each, as it takes its place in the family of nations, assumes it in all its plenitude. These rules the Government of this country has followed at all times and under all circumstances. Whatever may have been the sympathies of our people, whatever may have been the moral aspects of the foreign wars on which they have looked, and however much they have desired the success of one party over the other, they have inflexibly refused to throw their powers into the scale, or to allow any of their citizens to violate the neutrality which the Government enjoined. From the administration of Washington to the administration of Lincoln, through all the wars of the French Republic and the French empire, through the struggles of mastery in Eastern Europe, through the great civil wars in Poland, in Hungary and in India, we have steadily asserted the policy of non-interference, and maintained it in practice. And we have never resorted to the paltry evasion of doing secretly what we professed openly to avoid. What we said we meant, and what we meant we said. We have held the obligation to be paramount and universal. We complain of England and France, first for the proclamation or profession of neutrality, and then for the violation of the neutrality thus professed. This is not the place to enter upon the reasons which justify these complaints. The loyal people of this country have made up their opinions on both these subjects. They are convinced that England and France have wronged them in both respects, and are just as strongly convinced that Russia, whose naval officers are our guests to-night, has acted differently; has done us no injury; has conformed her conduct to the solemn injunctions of the law of nations, in accounting us competent to manage our own affairs; treating the established and recognized Government of the country as the only lawful belligerent, and holding no relations whatever with the rebels. It is impossible to mistake the settled convictions of the American people. They will never forget, through all the changes of future years, that in their mortal struggle the Czar has been true to them, and in the exercise of his great office has been inflexible in his adherence to the grand and salutary principles of public law. And they will just as surely never cease to believe that the Governments of England and France have desired the disruption of the republic, and have hastened unjustly to lift the rebels into the condition of legal belligerents; have offensively professed neutrality between the lawful and the rebel forces, and, after all, have evaded that professed neutrality by every species of indirect assistance which it was possible to give short of engaging in hostilities. *These things will never be forgotten so long as Americans can read and remember. And, more than this, the men of this generation, who have smarted under these wrongs, will not rest until some of them are righted.* We see the ground fresh with graves, half of which would never have been opened but for the countenance which England and France have given to the rebellion; and, whether it shall be procured from their apprehension of the consequences, or their sense of justice, *reparation must be made, or the seed which has been sown in these three years will ripen into an iron harvest of future war, of which no man can foresee the end.*

IF WE KNEW.
By Ruth Benton.

If we knew the cares and crosses
Crowding round our neighbor's way,
If we knew the little losses,
Sorely grievous, day by day,
Would we then so often chide him
For his lack of thrift and gain—
Leaving on his heart a shadow,
Leaving on our life a stain?

If we knew the clouds above us,
Held by gentle blessings there,
Would we turn away all trembling,
In our blind and weak despair?
Would we shrink from little shadows,
Lying on the dewy grass,
While 'tis only birds of Eden,
Just in mercy flying past?

If we knew the silent story,
Quivering through the heart of pain,
Would our womanhood dare doom them
Back to haunts of guilt again?
Life hath many a tangled crossing;
Joy hath many a break of woe;
And the cheeks, tear-washed, are whitest;
This the blessed angels know.

Let us reach in our bosoms
For the key to other lives,
And with love toward erring nature,
Cherish good that still survives;
So that when our disrobed spirits
Soar to realms of light again,
We may say, "Dear Father, judge us
As we judged our fellow-men."

Lector House believes that a society develops through a two-fold approach of continuous learning and adaptation, which is derived from the study of classic literary works spread across the historic timeline of literature records. Therefore, we aim at reviving, repairing and redeveloping all those inaccessible or damaged but historically as well as culturally important literature across subjects so that the future generations may have an opportunity to study and learn from past works to embark upon a journey of creating a better future.

This book is a result of an effort made by Lector House towards making a contribution to the preservation and repair of original ancient works which might hold historical significance to the approach of continuous learning across subjects.

HAPPY READING & LEARNING!

LECTOR HOUSE LLP
E-MAIL: lectorpublishing@gmail.com

Lightning Source UK Ltd.
Milton Keynes UK
UKHW010648090820
367908UK00002B/372